HEADLINES!
HEADLINES!

READ ALL ABOUT 'EM . . .
and Guess Which Actually Happened

HEADLINES?

FIGURE OUT WHAT'S NEWS . . . AND WHAT'S NOT!

Neil Patrick Stewart
Author of *Fact. Fact. Bullsh*t!*

▲adamsmedia
Avon, Massachusetts

Published by
Adams Media, a division of F+W Media, Inc.
57 Littlefield Street, Avon, MA 02322. U.S.A.
www.adamsmedia.com

ISBN 10: 1-4405-4010-1
ISBN 13: 978-1-4405-4010-3
eISBN 10: 1-4405-4386-0
eISBN 13: 978-1-4405-4386-9

Printed in the United States of America.

10   9   8   7   6   5   4   3   2   1

This publication is designed to provide accurate and authoritative information with regard to the subject matter covered. It is sold with the understanding that the publisher is not engaged in rendering legal, accounting, or other professional advice. If legal advice or other expert assistance is required, the services of a competent professional person should be sought.

—From a *Declaration of Principles* jointly adopted by a Committee of the American Bar Association and a Committee of Publishers and Associations

Many of the designations used by manufacturers and sellers to distinguish their product are claimed as trademarks. Where those designations appear in this book and Adams Media was aware of a trademark claim, the designations have been printed with initial capital letters.

Images © iStockphoto.com/tjhunt and bigstockphoto.com/scol22

This book is available at quantity discounts for bulk purchases.
For information, please call 1-800-289-0963.

BOOK FILLED WITH HILARIOUS HEADLINES, BOTH REAL AND FAKE, WILL MAKE YOUR HEAD EXPLODE—LITERALLY

Let's face it—newspapers are dying. Gone are the days when one would toss a nickel to a paperboy just to feel connected to the world. In the hyper-saturated, attention-deficit society of today, there are thousands of competitors for our attention. You're less likely to find someone reading an article about elections in Iraq than, say, Beyoncé's twitter feed.

So, what do news outlets do? They become entertainment *themselves*. That's why I wasn't shocked to turn on CNN one day and see a full news story about Obama's "swagga." (That's hip-hop parlance for "swagger" for you pop-culturally challenged.) Really, CNN?

It's the same story with the news in print. You don't open up *USA Today* or foxnews.com and expect to just read boring old stories about important stuff that's going on. You want excitement! Drama! Intrigue!

That must be why headlines are getting more and more ridiculous —they'll print anything just to get your attention. In this book, you'll find hundreds of humorous examples, from the truly weird ("Cupcake confiscated at airport, deemed security risk") to the totally dense ("Psychics predict world didn't end yesterday"), mixed up with some imitation ones, just to keep you on your toes.

On each page you'll find three headlines—two completely real and lifted from a legitimate news source, and one totally made up by me. Guess the fake and turn the page to find out if you're right.

You'll find that telling the difference is awfully hard—newspaper editors are just as good as I am at creating salacious, hysterical, and sometimes *titillating* titles to grab the eye. Enjoy!

AMAZING MILWAUKEE DOG PLAYS CHESS, CHECKERS

Dog wears pants, does something incredible

REAL! The headline appeared in the *Deseret News* in November 2011, and described the very unfortunate Brigham City duck hunter.

Wrapping up for the day, the man laid his shotgun on the bow of his boat and stepped out to gather some duck decoys. As he bent over to scoop them up, his dog promptly stepped on the gun and shot him in the butt.

Personally, I think the pooch did it on purpose.

FAKE! There is no dog intelligent enough to play chess. Yet. But if you thought it was true, I admire your optimism.

It reminds me of an old joke:

A man visits his friend's farm and is amazed to find him playing chess with his dog. "That's incredible!" he says. "Your dog must be incredibly smart!"

"Not *that* smart," said his friend. "I just beat him three out of five."

REAL! This bizarre headline appeared on the CBS News website in December 2011. It described a dog owner's amazement that, after he put Santa pants on his pup, it proceeded to walk around the house on his front legs *only*.

Really, CBS? This is news? If you tell me a dog does something incredible, I expect it to be truly incredible, like . . . well, like playing *chess*.

Tiger Woods plays with own balls, Nike says

MORE WOMEN FINGERED AS TIGER MISTRESSES

Cheating Tiger, Hidden Whore

REAL! The headline appeared in multiple local newspapers in 2000 as an unfortunately worded paraphrase of the original AP article headline: "Nike admits it: Tiger Woods doesn't use the balls he endorses."

Nike was successfully sued by the nonprofit group Public Remedies when it pointed out that Woods claimed to use "Nike Tour Accuracy" balls, when in fact he used his own custom-made golf balls.

Turns out that Woods prefers to play with firmer balls.

REAL! The writer of the 2009 Fox News headline was either glibly oblivious to the double entendre, or thoroughly aware and unapologetic of its salaciousness. Though funny, either explanation is unforgivable.

FAKE! While not an actual news headline, it *is* the headline of a 2009 blog entry on the website dlisted.com.

You can, however, find a bevy of truly brash and very real Tiger Woods headlines in the annals of the *New York Post*. My favorites:

Tiger admits: I'm a Cheetah.

Warning: Tiger on the loose. Lock up the waitresses.

Tiger goes limp!

Subtle, *New York Post*. Subtle.

Attorney challenged girl-friend to naked sword fight

25-YEAR-OLD IOWA MAN KILLS MOTHER'S BOYFRIEND WITH SWORD

GRANDMA DIES TRYING TO STOP SWORD FIGHT

REAL! Florida lawyer Terry Lee Locy was sick of his girlfriend suggesting that he quit drinking. Therefore, it's only natural that he step out of the shower one day, toss a sword to his girlfriend, and (allegedly) say, "You're going to need this," before pulling out a much larger sword of his own.

The 2011 headline and story appeared on NBC Miami's website and detailed the freaky fracas that ensued, during which the girlfriend escaped, mostly unscathed.

I'm surprised, though, that he armed her beforehand. No true lawyer would seek a fair fight. (That lawyer joke is for you, Uncle Anthony!)

FAKE! It's not far-fetched at all, though. The New York *Daily News* ran a nearly identical headline in 2011, as long as you replace the word "sword."

In truth, Bradley Arterburn of Oskaloosa, Iowa, killed his mother's boyfriend of three weeks with a medieval *battle axe*.

REAL! The 2009 headline appeared on MSNBC's website in reference to the sad fate of seventy-seven-year-old Franziska Stegbauer, who vainly tried to prevent her grandson and brother-in-law from engaging in a very real, full-on, no-holds-barred duel with swords.

She should have put on her chainmail first.

BREAKING NEWS

Bishops agree sex abuse rules

Girls' schools still offering 'something special'—head

Weiner comes from behind, wife happy

REAL! The April 2011 article from the *Sunday Business Post* details progress that the church is making toward eradicating sexual misconduct among the clergy, but the headline unfortunately omitted the crucial preposition "on," thereby implying that religious leaders find sex abuse to be *thoroughly awesome*.

Talk about Freudian slip.

REAL! It's certain that the writer of the February 2011 article in the *Gloucestershire Echo* did not mean to suggest that the local all-girls school provides oral sex as part of the program, though that would certainly qualify as "something special."

The journalist meant to say, of course, that the head of the girls' school believes that an all-girls education has a special quality that a coed education does not.

In truth, there is likely far less "head" going on at all-girls schools . . .

FAKE! Though there are a lot of plausible nonsexual scenarios that this headline could apply to, it was in fact made up.

However, the headline "Trojans come from behind against Beavers" is deliciously real.

Frosted cupcake sparks airport terror alert

CHICAGO WOMAN CHARGED WITH ASSAULT AFTER PELTING HUSBAND WITH CUPCAKES

BRITISH SPIES ATTACK AL-QAIDA BASE WITH EXPLODING CUPCAKE

REAL! The article from the *Daily Mail* relays the very sad story of Massachusetts college professor Rebecca Hains, who encountered tragedy when she went through the security line in the Las Vegas airport.

They took her cupcake.

The security agent told her that the frosting on the cupcake could be deemed a liquid or gel, and was therefore against carry-on rules. After a major media cupcake outcry, the TSA has condemned the decision, said it is reviewing the incident, and assured the public that cupcakes are acceptable on U.S. flights.

REAL! I could see making her pay the cleaning bill, but *assault* charges?

The 2011 article from Fox News describes how a domestic argument gone sour led sixty-year-old wife Dawn Montesdeoca to reach into a dessert box and begin to target her husband with a steady mortar fire of frosted cupcakes.

The police report indicated that she openly admitted to the "cupcake assault," and a county judge charged her with domestic battery and set her bail at $10,000.

Seriously?!

FAKE! While that *would* be awesome, British intelligence did something almost as awesome. They hacked into the website of an al-Qaeda magazine and replaced a bomb-making recipe with cupcake recipes.

If terrorists were obsessed with making cupcakes instead of bombs, what a wonderful world it would be.

ARIZONA COUPLE ADOPTS HAMBURGER, NAMES IT PETE

Gay penguin couple adopts

BREAKING NEWS

MAN ADOPTS GIRLFRIEND AS DAUGHTER

FAKE! It would make a great children's book, though.

REAL! The headline appeared on CBS Minnesota's news site in 2011 and refers to two male penguins at Harbin Polar Land in northern China who behave as a couple and were constantly trying to steal eggs from female penguins during hatching season.

Keepers gave the unruly pair an egg of their own so that they could experience the joys of joint fatherhood.

REAL! The 2012 article from KXLY in Spokane, Washington, tells the story of polo club magnate John Goodman (no relation) and his clever maneuvering to protect his assets from a lawsuit.

The wealthy Florida businessman allegedly killed a man by running a stop sign while drunk, and now faces a massive lawsuit by the victim's family. Goodman decided to man up and do the right thing: adopt his forty-two-year-old girlfriend, utilizing a sneaky legal loophole to protect his assets from the victims. Nice moves, Goodman. Nice moves.

100 PERVERTS ARE CHEMICALLY CASTRATED

Frat boy accidentally castrates self with beer bottle

MODEL CASTRATES CELEBRITY JOURNALIST WITH CORKSCREW

REAL! Did you know some countries force child molesters and rapists to undergo a chemical process that attempts to eliminate their sex drive? I didn't. Some U.S. states employ the practice as well.

This bluntly phrased 2012 headline from the *Sun* describes Britain's ongoing experiments with the technique. In the case of the United Kingdom, it is voluntary—offenders can opt to take the chemical castration drug leuprorelin in exchange for softer sentences.

FAKE! Luckily, this one isn't true, but I've known a couple of guys who've come close.

REAL! Media reports, such as this 2011 article from AsiaOne, describe what sounds like a happy Portuguese celebrity couple on vacation in New York City. Renato Seabra admitted to stabbing journalist Carlos Castro in the head with a corkscrew, using the corkscrew to mutilate his genitals, strangling him, smashing a computer monitor on his head, and stomping on his face many times. He then showered, put on a suit, and went out on the town leaving Carlos to die. What possessed the model to embark on the hourlong torture of his partner remains a mystery, but some media reports say that he did it in an attempt to banish the "gay demons" from his partner and himself.

DUNG IS PROMISED VERY ELEGANT DAY

Dung-lashed Catholics rate Rudy high

Malaysian drug addicts turn to cow dung

FAKE! That would certainly make for a strange story.

I didn't make it up out of whole cloth, though. This headline did appear in a 1945 issue of the *Pittsburgh Press*: "Ding is promised very elegant day."

At the time, the newspaper used a cartoon bird mascot named Donnie Dingbat to relay the weather. He was known as "Ding" for short.

REAL! The *New York Post* printed this strange headline in 1999. It refers to the fact that Mayor Rudy Giuliani's approval rating among white Catholics surged after he publicly condemned the Brooklyn Museum for featuring an artwork called "The Holy Virgin Mary."

The problem? The piece was made up of a few nontraditional materials, including oil paint, glitter, pornographic images, and elephant dung.

REAL! In 2004, Malaysia, which had earned a reputation for being hard on drugs, thought it had done a pretty good job getting drugs off the streets. It turns out they needed to look in the fields. As the *United Press International* article relates, addicts learned somehow that they could get some relief from withdrawal by putting cow dung in a bag, poking a hole in the bag, and inhaling deeply.

Let's hope our red-blooded, farm-raised, American youth don't discover this edgy trend . . .

FOOTBALL PLAYER SENTENCED IN CHALUPA INCIDENT

Taco Bell worker shot by chalupa gunner

MAN FIRE-BOMBS TACO BELL FOR MEATIER CHALUPA

REAL! I had some friends on the football team in high school that definitely had a "chalupa incident" or two, but not the kind that this Junction City, Kansas, *Daily Union* headline was referring to.

University of Kansas defensive end Dion Rayford found himself feeling a little miffed in 1999 when the local Taco Bell left a chalupa out of his order. Rayford did what any red-blooded rage beast would do: he rallied and rammed himself through the drive-through window. Unfortunately, he got stuck, and the police were called. Rayford was put on probation and had to miss the final game of his career.

All that for a chalupa.

FAKE! But, it is not far-fetched. In October of 2009, you may have seen this even better headline from NBC Miami: "Taco Bell worker shot by gordita gunner."

Sure, the drive-through jerk became enraged when he found out that the store was closing for the night. Yes, he pulled a gun and fired a shot at the unarmed, female manager through the window. But, is he known as the Queso Coward? No, he gets a cool supervillain name like the Gordita Gunner. Priorities, NBC, priorities!

REAL! According to the 2011 ABC News story, the customer called the restaurant around 4 A.M. "demanding more meat for his chalupas." The manager replied that they were closing and could not accommodate his request. He apparently responded, "That's alright. I'll just come redecorate the place."

Not long after, they smelled gasoline and found the drive-through area *on fire*. The police found the source: a Molotov cocktail.

Taco Bell is clearly the fast food of choice for mercenaries, bandits, pirates, and barbarians.

BREAKING NEWS

Leprechaun gang terrorizes mall

Leprechaun robs Butte laundry

LEPRECHAUN SHOT DEAD IN ST. PATRICK'S DAY SHOOTOUT

FAKE! Sounds like it could happen, though, right?

REAL! The 2005 story ran in the *Montana Herald*, and described a black-bearded, green-kilted little fella that made off with over $300 on the eve of St. Patrick's Day.

The owner of the laundromat, Don Heffington, apparently had a sense of humor about it all: "It is Butte. Butte gets pretty crazy on St. Patrick's Day, and it was probably someone who needed a little bit more money for stimulants."

REAL! The headline is from the United Kingdom's *Metro* newspaper, which detailed a bizarre 2010 bank robbery and its bloody aftermath in a suburb outside of Nashville, Tennessee.

A man dressed up as a leprechaun held up a bank teller with a high-caliber gun, making off with a sack of money (what, no pot of gold?). An accomplice was waiting in a getaway car, but they were pursued by police. The leprechaun managed to shoot and disable one police cruiser, but made a fatal error when he decided to ditch his car and dash off into a field. The men continued to fire at officers, which promptly got them shot and killed.

The robbers turned out to be baby-faced twenty-year-olds. Clearly they'd watched too many movies.

SEXUAL SPORTS

It's really not surprising that the language of sports only needs the slightest inadvertent adjustment to become the language of sex. After all, you can pull off a golden sombrero, ring the pipe, do some cradling, experience a back court violation, and "penetrate, penetrate, penetrate," without playing a sport at all.

HOOKER NAMED INDOOR ATHLETE OF THE YEAR

Sydney Morning Herald,
April 29, 2009

Before you think, "Wow, she must be *really good*," it's worth noting that the *Herald* was talking about pole-vault sensation Steve Hooker and the award he received from *Track and Field* magazine.

A-ROD GOES DEEP, WANG HURT

Plattsburgh, New York's
Press-Republican, June 16, 2008

Alex Rodriguez hit a three-run homer, and Chien-Ming Wang sprained his foot. What's sexual about that?

JUST ANOTHER DAY OF POUNDING, GETTING POUNDED

Iowa's *The Gazette*,
November 20, 2011

A rather philosophical piece about the physical toll taken on the University of Iowa Hawkeyes's bodies. All that grueling, sweaty grinding, and the constant ramming. It's tough on a guy.

COLON ABSORBS ANOTHER POUNDING; YANKEES MAY NEED WHIFF OF COLON; CLEVELAND'S COLON HAS EMERGED SMELLING LIKE A ROSE

The *Orange County Register*,
June 28, 2004; *USA Today*,
November 29, 2003; CNN/
Sports Illustrated, July 3, 1998

Newspaper editors have discovered endless opportunities for taking advantage of MLB pitcher Bartolo Colón's name.

CLINTON LICKS BEAVERS

Clinton, Tennessee's
Courier-News, **February 2, 2000**

Before you see the headline and say, "We knew that already," look more closely and see that the Clinton High School Dragons had a very successful basketball game against the Karns High School Beavers. Why the editor didn't choose "Dragons lick Karns" is a mystery to me.

LADY JACKS OFF TO HOT START IN CONFERENCE

Northern Arizona University's
The Lumberjack, **January 19, 2006**

It might take you a second to realize that women's teams at NAU are referred to as the "Lady Jacks." The basketball team was off to a strong start in their local conference with a big win over Weber State. Why, what did you think it meant?

FRESHMAN TALLEY MAKES BEST OF HER 2 SOGGY HOLES

Kentucky's *Courier-Journal*,
October 8, 2008

If you've got two soggy holes, you might as well make the best of them.

The article, of course, was a report of the Girls' State Golf Championships at Bowling Green Country Club. Wet weather mucked up the pitch, and competitors only played two holes. Emma Talley was the best, playing three under par.

OLD LADY UNABLE TO MASTER BATE AT HOME

Goal.com, December 10, 2008

I can't think of any *possible* way that the editor of this story thought people would read the headline and think it's about sports. Amazingly, however, it is. "Old Lady" is a common nickname for the Italian soccer team Juventus, and BATE Borisov is a Belarusian soccer team. In this case, as you can see, Juventus lost to BATE Borisov at a home game.

Teen steals bus, picks up passengers

TEEN STEALS TOMATO PLANT, MISTOOK FOR POT

Teen steals sex book, gets off

REAL! It's a rather fascinating story that Portland's KATU ran in 2006: a fifteen-year-old boy stole a bus, then proceeded to drive the standard route, obeying all traffic laws, while picking up and dropping off passengers at each bus stop.

He was arrested and charged with grand theft auto.

REAL! The 2012 story from Orlando's WESH stands as a real testament to teen intelligence: a woman came home just in time to witness a fifteen-year-old boy climbing out of her kitchen window with her tomato plant. The kid got away, but she happened to see him in the neighborhood the next day and called the police.

He admitted to the arresting officers that he took the plant, and that he did it because he thought it was marijuana. He did not mention whether or not he tried to smoke it.

Something tells me that kid's bought a lot of oregano in his life.

FAKE! It's not too far from the truth, however! In 1973, the *Pittsburgh Post-Gazette* ran a similar headline for the daily Ann Landers column. (For all you babies out there, Ann Landers was the name of a super popular syndicated advice column—people would write in for advice about everything from proper manners to ethical dilemmas.)

The headline read: "Teen steals sex book, gets off easy, but . . ." It referred to a very tame reader's letter about how she had attempted to shoplift a sex book when she was a teenager, and how the store manager had let her off with a warning.

Elderly golfers steal golf cart, travel 12 miles, fall asleep

ELDERLY GOLFERS BEAT TEENAGER FOR BLOWING AIR HORN

ELDERLY GOLFERS CAN BE SWINGERS

FAKE! Not real at all. It's the plot of a new buddy comedy I'm writing.

REAL! It's a classic prank. Wait until a golfer's at the peak of his wind-up, then blow an air horn. Pretty harmless, right?

Not for one teenager in Florida, according to this 2012 NBC News story. He and his buddies rattled two older golfers with an air horn and ran away laughing. His crucial mistake was returning to the course hours later to retrieve the jacket he left behind. The two golfers, both seventy-one, surprised the kid and beat the fifteen-year-old with a metal golf ball finder.

Both men were arrested and charged with *child abuse*. Never too old to get a record!

REAL! The 1981 piece from the *Boca Raton News* grabs your attention with its titillating title, then proceeds to bore the pants off of you with paragraph after paragraph of advice on how to improve your golf swing.

I did get momentarily excited when the article suggested using "a more supple shaft."

Former pro wrestler sues over lost testicle

WRESTLER SUES FOR FAULTY HAIRPIECE

Pro wrestler sues over stale Cocoa Pebbles

REAL! The wrestler, John Levi Miller, would not say that his case is funny at all. The 2012 NBC News story describes his bout one evening in a local Indiana circuit. He was supposed to win, and his opponent, Clinton Woosley, was supposed to be the "heel" and lose.

Miller's lawsuit claims that Woosley is a real-life heel who decided he wanted to win at all costs. He allegedly kicked Miller so hard in the groin that hospital doctors were forced to remove one of his testicles.

REAL! Pro wrestler Steve Thunder suffered "severe emotional distress" when his opponent ripped off his toupee in front of jeering crowds, according to his $200,000 lawsuit against Hair Replacement System. The 1983 article in the *Youngstown Vindicator* went on to say that Thunder "felt that his bald spots were ruining his career."

If you could successfully sue people because you're bald, I'd be a billionaire by now.

FAKE! I like the image of a massive man in spandex raging at his bowl of cereal. It's not so far from the truth, though. In 2010 pro wrestler Hulk Hogan did sue Post Cereal over a Cocoa Pebbles issue, but it was because the chocolate sugar bombs featured his likeness without permission.

BREAKING NEWS

MAN KILLED BY CONDOM

700-year-old condom discovered, historians "ecstatic"

Condom truck tips, spills load

REAL! Thirty-one-year-old Gary Ashbrook of Newhaven, East Sussex, England, had a truly bizarre way of achieving . . . gratification, as this 2007 headline from the *Daily Mirror* attests.

He was fond of inflating condoms with laughing gas and *stretching them over his head*. There's no way that habit was going to end any way but badly.

FAKE! But if it happens, they will be ecstatic.

In case you were wondering (I was), the oldest "surviving" condom is from 1640, and is made from pig intestine. It's a museum piece now and is even paired with an instruction manual in Latin.

REAL! The sassy headline appeared in the *London Free Press* in 2008 and has since gone viral, appearing on hundreds of joke-compiling websites.

However, the story itself is quite legitimate. Two huge tractor trailers collided on Highway 401 outside of London, Ontario. One, carrying hundreds of pounds of prophylactics, jackknifed and toppled over, dropping its contents onto the ground. As the writer of the article, April Kemick, noted, "the rubber truly hit the road."

PIGEONS CAN LEARN HIGHER MATH, STUDY FINDS

World's priciest pigeon goes for $328,000

DRAMA AT MANCHESTER AIRPORT AS PIGEON CLOSES RUNWAY

REAL! And from *The New York Times*, no less!

The 2011 article described a series of experiments that proved pigeons can count and learn rules about numbers just as well as monkeys can.

I thought it was funny that these pigeons were staring at a screen and pecking at symbols all day just to get a food reward . . . until I realized I'm doing the same thing.

REAL! The 2012 story from the *Wall Street Journal* describes the purchase by a wealthy Chinese shipping magnate of a Dutch pigeon, specifically bred for the sport of . . . pigeon racing. You can't make this stuff up.

The sport is popular in Europe, where it may be 2,000 years old, and has increasingly gained interest in China.

FAKE! This headline from the *Manchester Evening News* would be accurate if you replaced the word "pigeon" with the words "pink flamingo."

My favorite part of the story is that airport workers tried to secure the bird so that they could open the runway again, but the flamingo evaded them for *five* hours. That would make a great cartoon—sort of a cross between the Road Runner and the Pink Panther!

APPALLING FEET PROMPT POLICE RAID

Feds raid midtown strip club, receive lap dances

Federal agents raid gun shop, find weapons

REAL! The United Kingdom's daily *Metro* ran the headline, which refers to the consternation of German police in the town of Kaiserslautern, who broke into an apartment at the behest of a neighbor who believed he smelled a dead body. Instead, the police found a man who was very much living, despite his extraordinarily odorous feet.

FAKE! We all know that federal agents are far too responsible to do something like that. (While on duty, anyway.)

REAL! This is one of those headlines that was so disarmingly obvious that it went viral, and subsequently became a classic. It first appeared in the *Tulsa World* in 1997.

PREGNANT WOMAN BITES OFF HUSBAND'S EAR AFTER QUARREL

Wife bites off husband's tongue, then sings Christmas carols outside

BREAKING NEWS

Woman bites off husband's nose, demands beer

REAL! The 2011 headline from New Delhi TV's news website says it all. A woman named Shilpa was fed up with her husband and decided to take matters into her own . . . er, teeth. She made off with her husband's ear after a family fight.

The best part is the area of Mumbai that the woman is from: Diva.

REAL! The story, from New York's *Daily News*, describes how fifty-seven-year-old Sheboygan woman Karen Leuders decided to take off most of her seventy-nine-year-old husband's tongue during a goodnight kiss. While he was trying to relay his condition to a 911 operator (with extreme difficulty), she was outside caroling in the neighborhood. That's the spirit!

In a Herculean display of true love, the hubby didn't want to press charges. Wisconsin police pursued the case anyway.

FAKE! That would be violent and terrible.

It is awfully similar to an actual 2011 incident in Florida, reported by NBC Miami and the *Tampa Bay Times*: a massively drunk woman came home in a rage and demanded her car keys from her husband, who refused. When she opened the refrigerator and discovered that he'd thrown away the beer in an effort to protect her, she proceeded to bite him in the arm and neck four times, followed by a punch to the face for good measure.

BREAKING NEWS

Semen 'makes women happy'

2,000 attend 'semen party'

Horse-semen shots taste 'like custard'

REAL! The BBC News reported this exciting 2002 story about the effect that a man's seed can have on a woman's mood. The headline makes it seem as though just the very existence, or perhaps even the *idea*, of sperm makes the ladies smile, but the State University of New York study was more scientific than that.

Semen that has been deposited inside the vagina is absorbed into the body, the study notes, and it contains several hormones, notably testosterone and estrogen, that are proven to positively affect mood. Proof that sex (at least the unprotected kind) is a pick-me-up.

FAKE! *That* is an invitation that I would politely decline. In a 1942 edition of the *St. Petersburg Times,* you could have seen this header: "2,000 officers, men to attend seaman party."

REAL! You've really got to give it to the *Huffington Post* for running this headline in 2011, but you'd be surprised how many other reputable news sources carried versions of this story as well.

It's the utterly flabbergasting story of a New Zealand pub that offers apple-infused shots of horse semen on their menu, with the equally significant addition that the drink is very *popular*, particularly with women.

If you don't like apples, you're in luck. Elsewhere in New Zealand, you can find cherry-flavored and licorice-flavored horse semen as well.

Bogart, panda get boot after night club fracas

BOGART DOGS IRK WRITER

BOGART'S GANGSTA RAP QUIETS CRYING BABY

REAL! Dashing movie star Humphrey Bogart got caught up in a nightclub altercation, according to this story in a 1949 issue of the *Miami News*. Apparently, the actor decided to hit the town with two stuffed pandas in tow, which he had purchased for his young son.

This is where the details get murky. According to Bogart, fashion model Robin Roberts dashed up and tried to make off with one of the pandas, and he merely yanked it back. According to Roberts, she pet the toy panda, and Bogart knocked her to the floor.

The judge decided that it was an attempted publicity stunt by Ms. Roberts and threw out her charges of assault against him.

REAL! This 1953 item from the *Oxnard Press-Courier* tells the silly tale of a spat between Bogie and his neighbor, comedy writer Cy Howard. Bogart (and his lady, Lauren Bacall) had three Boxers that loved to bark all the time. Howard wanted them silenced; Bogart refused.

My favorite quote from the article belongs to Mr. Howard: "I work from home and if I have to write for Boxers, I listen to Boxers, but as long as I write for humans, the barking doesn't help."

Amen, brother!

FAKE! While we all know that Humphrey Bogart was not a gangsta rapper, "Bogart" could refer to aspiring rapper Evan Bogart or the music venue Bogart's. It could even be a reference to the town of Bogart, Georgia.

In the end, it's a riff on a real 2011 headline from Honolulu's KITV: "Biggie's gangsta rap quiets crying baby." It was an extremely worthy news item about how a father used rap songs to pacify his son with remarkable success. The "Biggie" in question, of course, is the late rap impresario Notorious B.I.G.

PANDA POO THE SECRET INGREDIENT IN WORLD'S MOST EXPENSIVE TEA

Aussies go crazy for cat poo coffee

Bar fined for serving liquor made from kangaroo poo

REAL! Chinese entrepreneur An Yanshi offers panda poop tea at more than $35,000 per eighteen ounces, according to this 2012 story from the *Huffington Post*. Why would you want to drink this fecal tea, which has been described as having a "nutty" and "mature" taste?

Apparently because pandas are rare, and their digestive systems are poor, so their poo-poo is riddled with nutrition.

Nummy!

REAL! Poop drinks seem to be all the rage! This 2007 Reuters article depicts Australian fascination with "Kopi Luwak," a special coffee from Indonesia.

The coffee is made entirely from coffee beans that are extracted by hand from the *feces of native civet cats*. Because this is such a time-consuming process, the coffee goes for more than $450 per pound!

I'm just waiting for it to appear at Starbucks.

FAKE! Stranger things have happened . . .

BREAKING NEWS

KILLER OFFERS SMURF DEFENSE

ROBBER DRESSED AS A SMURF ROBS CONVENIENCE STORE

Grandmother setup by a pot-pedaling Smurf?

REAL! The 2004 article in the *Lincoln Journal Star* chronicles the strange account of a Nebraska man on trial for murder, having shot and killed three people during his botched bank robbery. When asked why he started shooting, he claimed it was because a "Smurf was talking s#!t."

The county attorney asked, "Is it really your testimony that a blue Smurf was in the bank?"

The killer replied, "That's what I said."

He's now on death row.

FAKE! But, an almost identical headline ran online in 2011 by St. Louis's KSDK News: "Robber dressed as Gumby robs convenience store."

Turns out Gumby's a bum when it comes to the stickup: he fumbled in his costume for his gun, managing to drop thirty-seven cents in the process, before he took off.

I hold a special place in my heart for robbers who *lose* money . . .

REAL! The fact-checkers and copyeditors at Tampa Bay's WTSP News must have been playing hooky at Busch Gardens the day somebody decided to post this little gem. I have visions of a little blue man on a bicycle made of marijuana.

The headline is hilarious even when correctly rendered: "Grandmother set up by pot-peddling Smurf." It refers to a Pennsylvania woman who was arrested after several cannabis plants were found in her garden. Her delicious excuse is that a man in a Smurf hat gave her the seeds, which she then tossed into the garden and forgot about.

Right, grandma. Right.

BREAKING NEWS

NIPPLE DOCTOR VICTIM OF FIRE

Harry Nipple under arrest

Soviet nipple crisis solved

FAKE! I think putting the words "nipple" and "fire" in the same sentence should be avoided at all costs. Yet, against reason, I wrote it here. A 1954 headline in the *Prescott Evening Courier* read: "Whipple doctor victim of fire." The unfortunate Dr. Hipp, of the Fort Whipple Veterans Hospital, perished in a house fire.

REAL! According to this article in the *Atlanta Constitution*, there was, in fact, a living man named Harry Nipple in 1902, and he was *not* a good person. He was arrested for participating in a "lynching bee," which is just about the worst idea for a party that anybody has had. Ever.

REAL! Yes, the Soviet Union endured a nipple crisis. And thankfully, it was solved. The 1972 article in the *St. Petersburg Times* gave a detailed explanation as to how the superpower had been woefully underproducing "nursing nipples and pacifiers," then gleefully described the solution: "The key to the program is IRU-138, an experimental nipple-manufacturing machine with a potential output of 40 million nipples a year."

That is one impressive machine.

THIEVES STEAL . . .

Since the dawn of man, there have been footpads, filchers, and flim-flammers, ready to pinch, pilfer, and purloin anything they can get away with. A quick tour through news history reveals that *thieves steal the darnedest things*.

THIEVES STEAL MAN'S PROSTHETIC FOOT

Seattle's KING-TV News website, March 7, 2012

Is it possible to sink lower than that? Burglars raided Zac Vawnter's house and stole a laptop, a camera, and . . . a foot. It was designed for Vawnter and would be worthless to anyone else.

THIEVES STEAL BURGLAR ALARM FROM HOUSE

Schenectady Gazette,
April 26, 1963

The state-of-the-art system was designed to prevent crooks from getting in the house. A lot of good it did! The most unsettling part about

this one is that the thieves *didn't take anything else.*

THIEVES STEAL BEEF AND HAMS

Flushing Daily Times,
March 12, 1913

The subtitle: "Break window in Empire Market and get away with $20 worth of meat." And, in 1913, twenty dollars was, like, the equivalent of a *billion* dollars today . . .

THIEVES STEAL $1.5 MILLION WORTH OF CONDOMS

MSNBC, February 4, 2011

It was a sad day for Sagami Rubber Industries, one of the biggest purveyors of prophylactics in Japan. Over 700,000 condoms disappeared while they were being shipped in Malaysia.

THIEVES STEAL COOKIE MONEY FROM GIRL SCOUTS, HIT ONE WITH GETAWAY CAR

Fox News, March 4, 2012

What the . . . ? That's even lower than stealing a man's foot! It could be worse—the scout only suffered very minor injuries, and another scout managed to *punch a robber in the face* before he sped off. I hope she received a badge for that.

THIEVES STEAL AN ENTIRE ATM MACHINE

ABC News, December 24, 2011

It apparently happens all the time. Most run into trouble trying to get to the money itself. And, on a couple occasions, they've taken ATMs that were *out of money*.

THIEVES STEAL LOCAL BRIDGE

CBS Pittsburgh, October 7, 2011

It's outside the box, anyway. Officials in western Pennsylvania were scratching their heads when they discovered an entire *50-foot steel bridge* had been stolen. Two area brothers were busted when they sold the metal for $5,000 to a scrap dealer. The bridge was worth well over $100,000.

THIEVES STEAL WOMAN'S DRIVEWAY

Popular Fidelity, September 29, 2011

Yep, people will steal *anything*. The British robbers swiped the thousands of pounds of stone *in the middle of the day* while the owner was out shopping.

Hitchhiker dies from scrotum burns

'LEGAL' DRUG MEOW MEOW MADE MAN 'RIP HIS SCROTUM OFF'

Exposed: the myth of cello scrotum

FAKE! The headline may be bogus, but the gist is true. In 2008 the *Windsor Star* ran this story about an unconventional barbecue: "Hitchhiking marmot dies after scrotum burns." A cute little yellow-bellied marmot found himself black-bellied after riding for over 270 miles in the engine compartment of a minivan.

The poor guy had severe burns on his foot pads and scrotum, and was put down after it was clear he wasn't healing.

REAL! We can thank Britain's *Metro* newspaper for this bizarre-sounding and painfully descriptive lead. "Meow meow," in case you didn't know, is the street name for mephedrone, a drug sold legally over the Internet as plant fertilizer.

There has been a spate of hospitalizations as a result of young people testing out the drug, including the eighteen-year-old referred to here. After eighteen solid hours of hallucinating, the kid believed his testicles were being attacked by centipedes and decided to tear them from his body.

REAL! British paper *The Independent* eased musicians' minds with this illuminating 2009 exposé. It turns out a pair of British doctors had written a spoof letter to papers in the '70s about an unfortunate malady suffered by classical musicians, which they dubbed "cello scrotum."

A couple of reputable sources picked up the article as real, and the long-running legend of "cello scrotum" began. Thankfully, the nightmare is over.

BURGLAR ATE FAMILY GOLDFISH, AUTHORITIES SAY

Burglar breaks in, folds clothes, cooks dinner

BREAKING NEWS

BURGLAR WAKES MEN WITH SPICE RUB, SAUSAGE ATTACK

FAKE! It's my worst nightmare. They'll never get little Timmy.

REAL! I wish I had an intruder like that, about once a week.

The 2012 article from MSNBC goes on to paint a picture that's not quite as rosy. It's true that the South Bend, Indiana, trespasser folded the clean laundry he found, vacuumed, and then cooked up a nice chicken dinner.

But when the real owner came home, he yelled at her that it was his house, ordered her out, locked the door behind her, and relaxed on the couch until police arrived.

Stupid guy. If he had only welcomed her home and offered her some chicken, she may have asked him to stay.

REAL! It really doesn't get better than that. The 2008 story from ABC News explains that the intruder broke into the home of two farm workers, rubbed spices on the body of one sleeping man, and whacked the other with a sausage before fleeing.

Police found the man half-naked in a nearby field.

BREAKING NEWS

Raccoon BBQ leads cops to meth lab

Raccoon storms the field during Cowboys game

Raccoon sets fire to Arkansas church

REAL! As this NBC News headline helps illustrate: if you want to keep your brother's illegal methamphetamine laboratory a secret, you may not want to start roasting a raccoon in the parking lot of your shared apartment.

FAKE! Preposterous.

REAL! According to a 1966 issue of St. Petersburg, Florida's *Evening Independent*, a church cleaning lady dumped some burning refuse into a trash can, only to have a very startled furry fireball leap from inside.

The flaming rodent made nearly a full circuit of the building's perimeter before running away. Thanks to the property's lush, tall grass, the entire place was ablaze before people knew what was going on.

Nobody knows what happened to the rabid little fireball, but local residents say that sometimes, at night, you can still hear the squealing creature tearing its way through the underbrush, setting ghostly fires and stealing souls from the . . . oh, just kidding.

FRAT BOY SUES FOR INJURIES CAUSED BY ROCKET SHOT FROM ANUS

Woman goes for leg operation, gets new anus instead

YOUTH ABLE TO SEE WITH EYE TAKEN FROM ANUS

REAL! My favorite part of this 2012 story, which appeared in multiple newspapers (this headline is from the *Huffington Post*), is that the "frat boy" in question is not the owner of the "anus" in question. No, the plaintiff in this case was an "innocent" frat boy bystander, who claims he was so startled by his friend's butt fireworks that he jumped backward and fell off the deck that he was standing on. He sued for "pain and suffering," "medical expenses," and, my fave, "loss of time" from his baseball team, even though the deck was only 3 or 4 feet high.

Hmm, I wonder if this kid is pre-law?

REAL! Thank you, Fox News, for this glorious headline. It would be impossible to make up one as good as this. The 2008 story is an example of a classic trope: the old accidental hospital switcheroo. The poor German retiree went into a hospital in Bavaria for a leg operation and was mistaken for a woman with incontinence that needed surgery on her sphincter.

The article noted that the woman still needed a leg operation but was seeking a different hospital to do it. Wise.

FAKE! While I find that it delightfully boggles the imagination to think of what such a headline could possibly mean, it's made-up. The inspiration came from a 1937 headline in the St. Petersburg, Florida, *Evening Independent* that read: "Youth able to see with eye given by Amos."

It's the far-less-repulsive story of a successful corneal transplant.

Headless man robs barmaid

HEADLESS CHICKEN ENTERS TESTIMONY ON MERCY DEATH

HEADLESS BODY FOUND IN TOPLESS BAR

FAKE! Impossible. The idea came from a 1976 headline in the *Pittsburgh Post-Gazette*, which was less scary, more silly: "Bottomless man robs barmaid."

REAL! The strange sentence originates from a 1950 article in the *Milwaukee Sentinel*. A doctor was on trial for, essentially, "pulling the plug" on a terminally ill cancer patient after her heart had stopped. Prosecutors argued that because the patient was twitching, she was still alive.

Of course, an actual headless chicken did not sit on the witness stand and provide testimony—instead, the chicken was a hypothetical one (a beheaded chicken may twitch for some time after the chop) as the lawyers argued about what constitutes death.

REAL! One of the most famous funny headlines of all time, the 1983 story in the *New York Post* refers to the not-so-funny, gruesome murder and decapitation of a strip club owner.

After twenty-seven-year-old Charles Dingle shot the owner in the head, he proceeded to hold the dancers hostage, rape one, and rob them. He discovered from a business card that one of the strippers also worked as a mortician. He ordered her to behead his victim so that the bullet could not be traced to his gun. He then stole a cab and took two dancers and the head with him on a joyride, before he passed out at the wheel.

Dingle is still serving his life sentence in prison, and maintains his innocence.

Long Beach man beats up mom with rubber chicken

KIDS BEAT MOM AFTER SHE THROWS OUT BEER

Pasco County man uses eggnog bottle, stun gun to beat up his mom, deputies say

FAKE! Totally made-up. Rest easy. The Long Beach man, the mom, and the rubber chicken are all unharmed.

REAL! The CBS St. Louis story is quite disturbing. A mother throws out cans of beer that she finds in the fridge because her kids aren't old enough to drink. Kids find out, beat mom severely, leave her bleeding.

REAL! You can always count on the *Tampa Bay Times* for some good ones. The sick individual in question here didn't stop at the eggnog bottle and the stun gun. He also beat his elderly mom with *her own oxygen tank*.

BREAKING NEWS

U.S. puts bacon satellite in orbit

TRIBUTES PAID TO BACON RIND

Study: bacon an effective "nasal tampon"

FAKE! It's one word off from a true 1961 headline from the *Chicago Tribune*: "U.S. puts ham satellite in orbit." The "ham" in question, of course, is in reference to "ham radio," a common term for amateur radio. The satellite *Discoverer* had a 10-pound radio on it, which broadcast the message "Hi" to ham radio operators the world over.

A bacon satellite would be awfully fun, however.

REAL! The "Bacon Rind" in question is not an actual piece of food, but the completely legitimate name of a former chief of the Osage Indians. The headline appeared in the *Los Angeles Times* in 1932, after Bacon Rind passed away. He was a popular figure, and his memorial service was attended by people of all ethnic backgrounds.

REAL! If it weren't a bona fide headline, I never would have gotten away with including such a gratuitously strange phrase!

It's from St. Louis's *Riverfront Times* website and refers to a very real study from the *Annals of Otology, Rhinology & Laryngology*, which found that crafting a "nasal tampon" (the scientists' words) from cured, salted pork was an extremely effective way of curbing nasal hemorrhage.

Don't try this at home, kids. Doctors warn that bacon up the nose could provide bacteria and parasites with amazing access to your brain and lungs.

WOMAN SAYS PARROT ATTACKED HER AT CAR DEALERSHIP

Opera singing parrot lost in New York aria

JUSTIN BIEBER 'MARRIES' AVALANNA, SIX-YEAR-OLD AFRICAN GREY PARROT

REAL! The 2012 WLKY story describes a woman's claim to police that the mascot of a car dealership lunged at her and pecked her in the face. No charges were filed after eyewitnesses claimed the bird made no contact with the woman, and police noticed she had no marks, cuts, or bleeding at all.

REAL! It's the sad saga of Captain, a green Amazon parrot that was fond of singing and dancing and had the vocabulary of a two-year-old child. Captain became lost in New York in November 2011, and his owner was frantically trying to find him.

At least the editor at ABC News had a sense of humor about it, when she decided to forgo the word "area" in favor of the funnier, but far-less-accurate, word "aria." Nice moves, ABC. I see what you did there.

FAKE! You gotta give the Bieb a little more credit. He did stage a pretend marriage in 2012 with six-year-old Avalanna Routh, a Massachusetts cancer patient . . . and a human.

STUDENTS EXPELLED IN LAXATIVE CUPCAKE CAPER

Ex-Lax cookie stunt causes emergency plane landing

BREAKING NEWS

FIVE 8TH GRADERS CHARGED WITH LAXATIVE-LACED DOUGHNUT PRANK

REAL! The New Orleans *Times-Picayune* featured this 2008 story about one of those "it seemed like a good idea at the time" moments. Two seniors baked a batch of cupcakes with MiraLax in both the batter and the icing, and left them in the teachers' lounge at the Patrick F. Taylor Science and Technology Academy.

The police were called, and both students were expelled and faced charges related to poisoning that carried thousands of dollars in fines and potential jail terms of two years or more.

Both kids were honor students with spotless records both at the school and in the outside world.

Oops.

FAKE! It could have, though. In 2011, University of Wisconsin student Becky Riiser loaded a batch of cookies with a half-box of Ex-Lax and delivered them to the office of her extremely strict biology professor. Proving that she's extra devious, Riiser timed the delivery to coincide with an upcoming cross-country flight of the professor's.

Someone tipped off the teacher, and Riiser was expelled just as quickly as those cookies would have been.

REAL! Two thirteen-year-olds and three fourteen-year-olds found themselves in hot water, according to this 2007 Fox News story. The loaded doughnuts were ingested by nineteen students and a teacher before the trick behind the treats was revealed.

Many students had to go home, but not before the school nurse had a memorable day. The perpetrators were charged with the fake-sounding crime of "tampering with a consumer product."

If you've ever added sugar to your coffee, you may be guilty too.

Would-be Jedi jailed over lightsaber attack

DARTH VADER ARRESTED IN DENVER INDECENT EXPOSURE CASE

Drunken Yoda is caught by police

REAL! The MSNBC headline refers to the strange case of David Allen Canterbury, who went berserk at a Portland, Oregon, toy store in 2011, attacking customers with a toy lightsaber in each hand. He took his reign of terror out in front of the store, where he proceeded to swing at the police. He managed to deflect the officers' taser attack with his lightsabers before he was finally wrestled to the ground.

Canterbury received a sentence of forty-five days in jail. Easy time for a Jedi.

FAKE! It's totally something that he would do, though.

REAL! The 2011 story in Melbourne, Australia's *Herald Sun* described the surprise of German police in Darmstadt when they pulled over a driver for a hit-and-run and found him in a full-scale Yoda costume, green mask included.

What is surprising to me is the German police's sense of humor. In a statement they said, "The hapless Jedi returned home on foot. In this case, the force was not with him."

WOMAN OFFERED SEXUAL FAVORS FOR CHICKEN MCNUGGETS, POLICE SAY

'Pink slime' vanquished from U.S. McDonald's burgers

MCDONALD'S SUED OVER BIG MAC WITH SPIT

REAL! It's from a January 2012 *Los Angeles Times* article, which describes a Burbank woman's outside-the-box strategy for obtaining some lunch: walk along the line of cars at a McDonald's drive-through, open each door, and offer the startled driver a good time.

Personally, I would at least ask for some fries too.

REAL! This headline from *MacLean's Weekly* in Canada is just one example of a flurry of articles about McDonald's decision to scrap a very strange goo from their burger recipe: fatty beef trimmings (all sorts of weird animal by-product normally used in pet food) mixed with ammonium hydroxide (a strong chemical normally used in cleaning products).

Perhaps they'll begin to sell it separately in ketchup packets?

FAKE! However, the headline "Burger King sued over Whopper with spit" did appear in the United Kingdom's *Sky News*. McDonald's has had to contend with allegations of far worse things appearing in their food over the years, including (but not limited to): a 6-inch wire brush embedded in the meat of a Chicken Legends sandwich, a needle in a burger, both a condom and a Band-Aid in orders of fries, a rat in a salad, and my personal favorite—a fried, breaded chicken head in a box of wings.

Penis size linked to finger length

LARGE PENIS SIZE LINKED TO LOWER INTELLIGENCE, SAYS STUDY

BREAKING NEWS

SON'S PENIS SIZE WORRIES MOM

REAL! Just when we thought we'd put the hands- and feet-comparison myths about penis size to bed, this new study from Korea pops up in a 2011 ABC News story.

The catch here is that it's not about overall hand size, but about the ratio of the length of a man's ring finger when compared to his index finger. The study suggests that men whose ring finger is the same length or longer than his index finger is more likely to be well-endowed. The researchers attribute both longer relative ring finger size and larger penis size to being exposed to more testosterone while in utero.

The article noted that a separate study of ring-finger to index-finger ratio found that women with longer relative ring fingers were more likely to be lesbians.

Things that make you go "Hmmm."

FAKE! It's utterly and unequivocally untrue. Trust me.

REAL! We can get used to Mom worrying over just about anything, but this is taking it too far.

Unfortunately, the perturbed progenitress in this 1992 *Pittsburgh Post-Gazette* column was not concerned about what her son had between his legs, but with what he *lacked*. In fact, she wrote in to the newspaper that her twelve-year-old boy was outmanned by his six-year-old brother, and went on to equate Pee-Wee's pee-pee with that of a toddler.

I'm sure her profound anxiety and willingness to tell the world had absolutely no negative effect on her poor kid. And if he's reading now, I'd point him to the numerous recent studies that claim that men seem to care about penis length *much, much more* than women do.

NJ woman charged in penis silicone injection death

'DOCTOR' ACCUSED OF INJECTING WOMAN'S BUTT WITH CEMENT

Texas nurse accused of injecting orange juice into patient's foot

REAL! The 2011 ABC News article tells the sad tale of Justin Streeter, a twenty-two-year-old New Jersey man who attended a "pumping party" in hopes of enlarging his pee-pee. He accepted a silicone injection by a pretty, thirty-something doctor, Kasia Rivera.

Streeter died the next day of a silicone clot in his lungs, probably around the same time he started to wonder if Rivera was a real doctor.

Nonencapsulated silicone is only approved for injection around the eyes (a.k.a. Botox), and no, Rivera, who was charged with criminal manslaughter, is not a doctor at all.

REAL! We've got an epidemic on our hands. The *Miami Herald* story describes how transgendered pretend-doctor Oneal Ron Morris allegedly injected cement, mineral oil, and Fix-a-Flat into a woman's rear end and sealed it up with super glue.

The female patient, who wound up with a massive infection that threatened her life, had just wanted a bigger booty.

FAKE! C'mon. That's too weird.

Teacher guilty of abuse in hot sauce soda case

SPECIAL EDUCATION TEACHER ACCUSED OF USING HOT SAUCE ON STUDENTS

SCHOOL BOARD TRUSTEE ACCUSED OF HOT SAUCE THEFT

REAL! The 2009 NBC News headline describes how special needs teacher Sylvia Guadalupe Tagle spiked her soda with hot sauce in order to teach the kids not to take things from her desk. She was found guilty of child abuse.

REAL! There must have been a memo about the "Tabasco Technique." This time, Kissimmee, Florida, teacher Lillian Gomez was accused of applying hot sauce to crayons to teach her autistic kids not to put them in their mouths, according to this 2012 headline from NPR's website.

FAKE! But it's not far off. In 2008, you may have seen the slightly less spicy headline: "School board trustee accused of ketchup theft." Apparently, the offending gentleman tucked a bottle under his shirt after a meeting and walked out the door.

BREAKING NEWS

Penguin couple get married

'Skateboarding penguin' dies in skateboarding accident

Roast Beef the penguin charms nursing-home residents

REAL! The Shanghai Ocean Aquarium staged the ceremony for Valentine's Day 2012, the *Sky News* story reports. The loving couple, Xiaobai and Xiaoxue, were wed with wreaths of flowers as their trainer, Ding Ding, looked on.

It makes sense to me. Penguins are, after all, serially monogamous. It's about time they had access to marriage, instead of being relegated to insulting "civil union" status.

FAKE! Aren't you glad he's not dead? Except he doesn't exist, so that's kind of like being dead.

REAL! The real ones are always better than the made-up ones, aren't they? The story, from *Today*'s website, describes the thirteen-year-old African penguin from the New England Aquarium and his penchant for entertaining kids, and now the elderly too.

My favorite is how the article points out that Roast Beef has to remain inside his air-conditioned cube during visits, because of his ability to "projectile poop at any time."

POLICE KILL NINJA-CLAD, ARMED MINISTER

Ninja hamster in bloody attack

Man allegedly wounded by two 'booty call ninjas'

REAL! The *Pittsburgh Post-Gazette* spun the 2001 tale of Lynnport's Robert W. Furler, a Lutheran minister with his own congregation who engaged in a standoff with police after he refused to be committed for mental health issues.

Nearly twenty-four hours after the stalemate began, Furler had a bright idea to resolve the conflict. Just before dawn, the minister emerged from his house in full ninja garb, carrying two semiautomatic weapons, a long-barreled shotgun, and a *sword*. The officers on the scene ordered him to drop his mini-arsenal, but he instead leveled his shotgun directly at them. He was shot twice and pronounced dead at the hospital.

FAKE! It's a real 2011 headline from *The Sun*, if you just replace the word "ninja" with the words "kung fu." That's right. There was a bloody kung fu hamster attack. Be afraid.

REAL! Joliet, Illinois's *Herald-News* ran this bizarre headline in 2011.

The victim's only crime in the story was to call his ex-girlfriend late one night and ask for sex. The ex-girlfriend's crime, however, was a little more involved. After she agreed, she suggested he meet her out in the alley. When he arrived, the ex-girlfriend and a masked man jumped out of the shadows *with nunchucks* and proceeded to beat him up.

KLAN PLANK IN, M'DOO OUT, IS NOW PREDICTION

Fizzle-Hop Doo-Nut Shop opens for business

BEEZOW DOO-DOO ZOPITTYBOP-BOP-BOP ARRESTED

REAL! It's a real headline, from a ninety-plus-year-old issue of the *Baltimore Sun*. It refers to the 1924 Democratic National Convention, in which the Ku Klux Klan was actually an influential force and William Gibbs McAdoo (a.k.a. M'Doo) was a contender to be the Democratic nominee for president.

FAKE! But somebody make it real. Please. Make it real.

REAL! MSNBC reported this delightful story when Mr. Zopittybop-Bop-Bop was taken by the Madison, Wisconsin, police department.

Perhaps Jeffrey Drew Wilschke legally changed his name in an attempt to clear his record, since he'd been arrested a few months earlier for carrying a concealed handgun in a local park. It didn't work—when police found "Doo-Doo" in the park again, this time with a concealed knife and marijuana, they took him right back to jail.

MAN GROWS THIRD EAR ON FOREARM, SCIENTISTS STUMPED

Baby born with second penis on his back

BREAKING NEWS

Woman with two vaginas offered $1m to make porn movie

FAKE! There is, in fact, a grown man out there with an ear on his forearm, but scientists aren't stumped about it at all. That's because performance artist Stelios Arcadious had a surgeon implant the ear in his arm *on purpose*.

Because that's not weird enough, Arcadious is working toward implanting a Bluetooth microphone in his third ear so that people can listen to everything his arm "hears."

REAL! It's terrifying, but true. Australia's *Daily Telegraph* reported this story of a Chinese baby, born in May 2008, with one perfectly normal penis, and a second, slightly less normal penis positioned in the exact center of his back.

The kid is not an extraterrestrial—he was just a victim of a developmental abnormality called "fetus in fetu." Doctors removed the little surprise from the baby's back in a three-hour surgery and pronounced him perfectly healthy and normal.

REAL! *The Sun* ran the headline in 2012, and countless other news sources reported the story. The woman in question, Hazel Jones, has a condition called "uterus didelphys," and has a double uterus, two cervices, and two vaginas.

Porn giant Vivid Entertainment made her the million-dollar offer, which she declined.

Girl marries ghost

MAN MARRIES GIRL DEAD FOR 18 YEARS

SWEDISH CANNIBAL, SATANIC VAMPIRE TO BE MARRIED BEHIND BARS

FAKE! Sorry to break it to you: ghosts aren't real. Louisville, Kentucky's *Courier-Journal* did run a multipart, serialized short story called "Girl Marries Ghost"—so the headline is technically real, though certainly not *true*.

REAL! The rather macabre headline ran in a 1962 issue of the *Reading Eagle* and described how a Taiwanese man decided he needed to be granted a "spirit wedding" to the long-deceased daughter of his tailor. He claimed she appeared to him in a dream and told him that "he would not regain his health until he married her."

Amazingly, her parents agreed to the wedding and threw a lavish wedding feast.

REAL! This headline from the *International Business Times* is perfectly succinct. You get most of the information you need directly from the title!

Both Isakin Johnson, who beheaded his former girlfriend and proceeded to eat parts of her body, and Michelle Gustaffson, who stabbed a man to death and drank his blood, are inmates-for-life at a high-security mental hospital in Sweden. They fell in love while chatting through an online message system (WHY are these guys allowed online?), and the hospital is actually considering their request.

Woman charged with stealing underwear, cheese

WOMAN CHARGED WITH STEALING BULL SEMEN

Woman charged with stealing husband's coffee

REAL! Stranger things have certainly happened, but this 2010 *Springfield News-Sun* headline is perfectly constructed for producing a chuckle.

The woman in question, Ashlie Green of Urbana, Illinois, allegedly attempted to walk out of a local Walmart with not only underwear and cheese sticks, but also body spray and "silly bands."

You know . . . the necessities.

REAL! You might think, "Who would want to steal bull semen?" I certainly did. Well, according to the CBS News article, the stolen goods in this story were worth more than *one hundred thousand dollars* because the bull was from fine breeding stock.

FAKE! I can think of multiple occasions where my wife was guilty of that. The fake headline was inspired by an even better real one from the *Atlanta Journal-Constitution*: "Woman charged with spiking husband's coffee." The woman loaded up her hubby's morning drink with Xanax, she claimed, to calm him down. She was charged with attempted felony murder.

CANNIBALS!

Throughout the history of newspapers, editors have learned that there aren't many attention-grabbing words as potent as "cannibal." Naturally, they jumped to use it when they could. Here are some of the oddest examples.

GOLDFISH TURN CANNIBAL BECAUSE OF KIND OLD LADY

Milwaukee Sentinel,
September 29, 1941

It seems they had a problem in Crystal Lake in the San Gabriel Valley with goldfish turning predator and attacking/eating other fish in the lake. The goldfish had been introduced because the "kind old lady" was moving back east and dumped her fish in the lake. Still, I doubt the fish became murderous *because* of grandma.

CANNIBAL KUDOS HARD TO SWALLOW

Milwaukee Journal, **August 10, 1977**

There was a bit of a fuss when a "name the cafeteria" contest in a government building resulted in it being dubbed the Alfred E. Packer Grill. The problem? Packer was a nineteenth-century pioneer who was charged with—and convicted of—cannibalism. The article quoted the judge from his 1874 case: "There was only six democrats in all of Hinsdale County, and you, you man-eating S.O.B., you ate five of them. I sentence you to hang by the neck until you're dead, dead, dead, as a warning against the further reducing of the democratic population of this county."

HIPPIES CHARGED WITH MURDER IN CANNIBAL CASE

Hartford Courant, **July 16, 1970**

I think the editor of the *Courant* had it out for hippies. The people-eaters in this case were reclusive, unwashed Satan worshippers in a Yellowstone campsite, but they don't sound like hippies to me. The killers blamed their crime on drugs, thunder, lightning, and a demonic trance.

MAN-EATING JAPS CONFESS CANNIBAL ORGIES IN PHILIPPINES

Los Angeles Times, **June 9, 1947**

It's an absolutely horrifying tale of a group of thirty-one Japanese soldiers that roamed the jungle in the Philippines, attacking and consuming innocent victims, and sometimes each other. The captured soldiers admitted that the cannibalism began because of malnutrition, but evolved into a mad obsession.

claim that, in order to fit in, he had to sample human flesh, which, he reported, was tasty. He wrote, "Cannibal land is as safe for the well-behaved man as New York."

CHARLESTON DANCE SAVES LIFE OF CAPTIVE OF CANNIBAL TRIBE

**Boston Daily Globe,
March 15, 1927**

Truly, it sounds like a Charlie Chaplin movie. A British composer was visiting Epi Island in the New Hebrides and, according to multiple newspapers, was captured by cannibals. He staved off their attack by dancing the Charleston, and then teaching it to them. The tribe showered him with gifts and escorted him to safety.

AUTHOR, GUEST OF CANNIBAL KING, SAYS HUMAN FLESH TASTES LIKE VEAL

**Lewiston Morning Tribune,
April 2, 1931**

New York author William Seabrook claimed to have spent six months among the "Guere" cannibal tribe in western Africa. He went on to

Amish driver wins National Hot Rod Association drag racing championship

Amish man charged with sexting, soliciting minor for sex in his buggy

Ohio Amish attacked by beard- and hair- cutters

FAKE! Everybody knows that the Amish can't drive *cars*. BUT, in 2011, you may have seen this AOL News headline: "Plenty of Horsepower: Amish man accused of drag racing in buggy."

The street race, in Ashland, Ohio, was between two Amish drivers in two horse-drawn carriages. One got in trouble with the police when he attempted to pass his compatriot in the oncoming-traffic lane. To where were the two buggies racing?

Church.

REAL! It turns out you can find perverted weirdos in *every* culture. The episode, as printed by *USA Today*, involved twenty-one-year-old Willard Yoder, of Milroy, Indiana, allegedly sending more than 600 graphic texts, photos, and videos to a *twelve-year-old girl*.

Cops said that Yoder drove his buggy to meet her for sex, but clip-clopped into their trap instead.

REAL! The most fascinating part of this 2011 story from ABC News is that the gang that was surrounding Amish men and attacking them with scissors and trimmers is thought to be a "formerly Amish cult." The string of attacks occurred in several counties in Ohio and prompted the victims to do something that is not the norm in their culture: press charges.

The article quoted Elizabethtown College professor Donald Kraybill as saying, "Amish-on-Amish violence is extremely rare."

Scary times.

BREAKING NEWS

Babysitter bites off penis of urinating boy

Texas woman bites off own child's penis

Secretary accidentally bites off boss' penis

FAKE! Inspiration came from an equally eye-catching 2000 headline in the *New Straits Times*: "Donkey bites off penis of urinating boy."

A fourteen-year-old kid in Kano, Nigeria, was peeing against a wall when the donkey next to him snapped his manhood between its jaws, severing the tip. Doctors reported that after a few surgeries, the boy's penis would be functional.

REAL! As the horrifying 1996 story in the *Manila Standard* reported, a Fort Hood woman bit off her four-year-old son's penis, then proceeded to strangle and suffocate her two-year-old son.

Police responded to a disturbance call after screams were heard from the residence and found the woman with her face buried in the "buttocks area" of her two-year-old.

The two-year-old died, and the four-year-old's penis was never recovered.

REAL! According to the *Malaysia Star*, a husband suspected his wife of cheating and had her followed by an investigator.

The investigator watched as the scene unfolded: the woman and her boss stopped at the park in a van. They both went in back of the van, which eventually started to rock perceptibly. Suddenly, a car came out of nowhere and rear-ended the van. Screams followed, and the woman appeared, her mouth covered in blood.

The private eye called the ambulance, which took the man to the hospital, but they forgot something important: his severed penis.

The woman got her wits about her and drove the penis to the hospital so that it could be reattached.

That night, her husband got one heck of a report from the investigator!

WOMAN BURNED BY FLAMING CHERRIES JUBILEE SUCCUMBS

Tableside Bananas Foster goes awry, flames burn four

BREAKING NEWS

CHILD BLINDED BY BAKED ALASKA EXPLOSION

REAL! It's not how grandma wanted to go. An elderly patron of a Coral Gables country club died from burns she received after her cherries jubilee exploded and set her on fire, according to this 1979 article in the *Los Angeles Times*.

REAL! You could say dinner ended with a bang for four friends at Palm Harbor's Ozona Blue restaurant. The 2011 *Huffington Post* article explains that the typical final flourish of tableside Bananas Foster preparation is to set it on fire. However, on this particular night, the waiter accidentally added too much rum.

The resulting conflagration set all four diners alight. Two were released with minor burns, but two had to be flown to Tampa General Hospital for serious injuries.

FAKE! Never happened. But, according to a 1976 report in the *Ocala Star-Banner*, four people were rushed to the hospital when a waiter accidentally set them on fire when he walked by with a flaming Baked Alaska.

You've heard it before, and I'll tell you again: *dessert is not good for you!*

Greek ruler dead from monkey bite

FERAL MONKEY DISCOVERED IN RHODE ISLAND TEENAGER'S BEDROOM CLOSET

KUNG FU MONKEYS ATTACK CAMERAMAN

REAL! History buffs recognized this one. The headline is from a 1920 issue of the *Milwaukee Sentinel*, and it's reporting the very true, very bizarre death of Alexander of Greece.

While walking him through the royal gardens, Alexander's dog was attacked by two monkeys. The monarch defended his dog with a stick, but received a series of bites for his trouble. One cut opened a gland, and the monkeys turned out to be diseased. Alexander died a few days later of sepsis.

His father, Constantine I, returned to power and eventually started the Greco-Turkish War, which was a disaster for Greece. Winston Churchill later wrote that "it was a monkey bite that caused the death of those 250,000 people."

FAKE! Fans of *Family Guy* will have recognized this as a running gag from the animated series.

REAL! *The Sun*'s decision to run this headline in 2010 is a perfect example of sensationalism. In truth, the cameraman in question managed to snap some photos of lemurs jumping around in kung fu–like poses.

GEORGIA DEER CRASH LANDS IN MEXICAN RESTAURANT

Robo-deer join fight against poachers

FLORIDA DEER WINS BATTLE WITH BURMESE PYTHON

REAL! According the the ABC News story, customers at the Taco Mac outside Atlanta were minding their own business, eating and watching the football game, when a large buck crashed *through the front window* and cantered around the restaurant in a panic. It made its way out the back door, and then turned around and tried to *get back in*, headbutting the door several times. Finally, it hopped a fence and ran away.

Apparently, this kind of thing is not so rare. The article alludes to a deer in New Jersey that crashed through a mall window and went into a Journeys shoe store and two fawns in Suwanee, Georgia, that ran into a Publix.

I think this is a sign. Watch out people—the deer-pocalypse is coming.

REAL! The headline, from the *Tampa Bay Times*, refers to a collection of mechanical deer that the Utah Division of Wildlife Resources uses to catch poachers in the act. The program is so successful that one robo-deer had to be retired after being shot *one thousand times*.

FAKE! In fact, the deer lost in a decisive fashion, as you would expect. Massive snakes in the Everglades have been hunting deer with success.

In fact, in 2011 a 15-foot Burmese python was found with an intact 75-pound adult female deer *in its belly*. The deer-stuffed snake had a girth of 44 inches.

Two headed baby sometimes awake, asleep at same time

SPACEMEN MAY COME BACK WITH TWO-HEADED OFFSPRING

TWO-HEADED MOSQUITOES: NEW JERSEY FARMER ALARMED BY REPORT THAT SOME ARE BEING MANUFACTURED

REAL! The 1954 story in the *Milwaukee Journal* describes Donald Ray and Daniel Kaye Hartley, who would have been more aptly described as two conjoined babies, as opposed to one two-headed baby.

Such a circumstance has occurred multiple times in modern history. For example, Abigail and Brittany Hensel, of Minnesota, are dicephalic parapagus twins, and healthy adults. Each has a head, heart, lungs, and one arm, and they share a torso, pair of legs, large intestine, and one set of reproductive organs. As for outward appearances, they seem to be one two-headed person, when in reality they are two conjoined twins.

REAL! The 1966 article in the *Fort Scott Tribune* was clearly meant to be alarming, but was a cover for a slightly less shocking reality.

The astronauts of Gemini 8 brought pregnant frogs with them into space to determine how weightlessness affects development and birth. That the frogs may produce two-headed tadpoles was only conjecture.

FAKE! But not *that* fake. This was a trick one: in 1898, this exact headline appeared in the *New York Times*, with one slight difference. The mosquitoes were *three-headed*.

BREAKING NEWS

GIs concentrate on red booty

Astros, moon booty off to Hawaii

Baghdad plunged into booty darkness

REAL! While a modern reader might have images of soldiers staring at a crimson rear end, readers of the *Chicago Tribune* article in 1970 would have understood the true meaning first: American forces in Cambodia were looking to destroy or confiscate anything of value that the enemy, the communist Khmer Rouge, might claim.

REAL! "Astros" is short for "astronauts," and the "moon booty" was the 245 pounds of lunar samples that the crew of Apollo 16 were able to bring back from space, according to this 1972 article in the *Deseret News.*

After splashdown in the Pacific Ocean, the astronauts and the remainder of the spacecraft were picked up by the USS *Ticonderoga* and taken to Hawaii, hence the headline.

FAKE! I don't know what "booty darkness" is, but I'm sure I wouldn't like it. This headline from the *San Francisco Chronicle* would be accurate, were it not for one letter: "Baghdad plunged into sooty darkness." That makes a heckuva lot more sense.

JUDGE EXACTS BLOOD FROM 69 CRAP SHOOTERS

Big Apple flap over Madonna slap crap

BREAKING NEWS

CRAP REMOVAL IS CANCELED

REAL! While the headline seems scarily macabre, the story from a 1951 issue of the *Eugene Register-Guard* was actually quite positive. When faced with the sixty-nine men arrested at a busted $20,000 game of craps, the judge decided to get creative with the punishment. He ordered the men to report to the Red Cross and donate blood to support the American soldiers in Korea.

All sixty-nine men happily agreed.

REAL! The columnist behind this 1999 headline in the *Chino Valley Review* was clearly feeling slaphappy when he penned this one.

The article is about the outrage at artist Chris Ofili's work "The Holy Virgin Mary," which is a sculpture of St. Mary made out of elephant dung. The piece became one of the most controversial ever, due to the perceived insult inherent in using crap as a primary material. The artist maintained that the material wasn't meant to be provocative, and that manure is an earthy material that relates to his African heritage.

FAKE! The correct headline of the 1972 article in the *Milwaukee Sentinel* is "Carp removal is canceled." Therefore, we can all be happy to know that Milwaukee endured no interruption in their crap removal that year.

Doritos creator dies, to be buried with chips

PRINGLES CAN INVENTOR BURIED IN PRINGLES CAN

INVENTOR OF THE CHEESE PUFF BURIED WITH 'ORANGE DUST' ON FINGERTIPS

REAL! Arch West, the inventor of the cheesy corn chips, was so enamored of his creation that he ate them daily. In a strange, yet sweetly sentimental, tribute to the man, his family *sprinkled Doritos onto his body* during his burial. The Associated Press story with this headline was picked up by hundreds of newspapers in 2011.

REAL! The *Huffington Post* headline puts it quite succinctly. Chemist and "food storage technician" Fred Baur came up with the idea for stacking chips and storing them in a tube in the '60s, and in 1970 received a patent for the Pringles can.

He was so proud of his invention that he requested to be cremated, and for his ashes to be buried inside one of the iconic tubes. The family had a debate over which flavor of Pringles can to use, but finally settled on the poetic choice:

"Original."

FAKE! I love to imagine a nutty Doc-Brown-esque inventor of the cheese puff, and that he'd have a big enough sense of humor to be buried with cheesy residue on his fingertips, but alas, it's all fiction. In fact, history is too clouded for us to even identify the saint who came up with this glorious snack food—there are competing accounts, and no consensus as to where they originated.

I think it was Martians.

BREAKING NEWS

Steel mill spatula kills two

SPACEWALKERS LOSE A SPATULA, GAIN SOME CONFIDENCE

Greek doctors sentenced for leaving spatula in patient

FAKE! What exactly would a "steel mill spatula" be, exactly? Just a giant, industrial spatula that swings around scraping things? This falsie was inspired by a 1967 article in the *St. Joseph Gazette*: "Steel mill ladle kills 2; 29 hurt." It seems a huge dipper filled with molten pig iron came crashing down, splashing workers with 2800°F liquid metal. Talk about a bad day at the office.

REAL! Right now, somewhere in the vast, cold emptiness of space, a lone spatula is going where no spatula has gone before. It's just tumbling along, forever, in the frictionless void, a strange emissary of planet Earth.

Waco, Texas, news station KWTX printed the headline in 2006, which describes how astronauts Piers Sellers and Michael Fossum accidentally lost the intrepid spatula while performing maintenance on the outside of the *Discovery* space shuttle.

NASA wasn't mad. In fact, the spacewalk was considered a rousing success because Sellers and Fossum successfully pioneered a new shuttle repair technique.

REAL! Forget a slap on the wrist. In 2008, a Greek gynecologist, two doctors-in-training, and a scrub nurse were sentenced to *jail time* for accidentally leaving a 9-inch metal spatula inside a woman's abdomen, according to this article in the *China Post*.

The poor lady had just gone in for minor surgery.

Beaufort kazoo factory explodes

MAN SEIZED IN KAZOO SHOOTING

There are thousands of sad kazoo players

FAKE! There would be nothing funny about that. Kazoos unequivocally make the world a better place. You'll be happy that the real version of this 2010 headline by Charleston, South Carolina's WCSC bore news that was much more positive: "Beaufort kazoo factory expands despite economy."

Believe it: silliness is recession-proof.

REAL! Residents of southern Michigan would immediately point out that "Kazoo" is a popular abbreviation for Kalamazoo. As a result, throughout the years you may have seen a bevy of double-take-inducing headlines from area papers, like this one from a 1936 issue of the *Owosso Argus-Press*.

Others include: "Grocery clerk quizzed regarding two Kazoo deaths," "One dead in Kazoo plane crash," and "Double probe opens at Kazoo."

REAL! This soulful, existential, and deeply wise headline was run by ABC News in 2007. While I think the writer was making a profound social comment, the article explained that 2,500 kazoo players showed up to the Macon, Georgia, fairgrounds to hum "Take Me Out to the Ball Game," and set a Guinness World Record.

Unfortunately for the kazoo keepers, the previously set record was 2,700, and they went home in shame.

Scientists track penguin poop from space

PLANE
POOP
HITS
COUPLE

THE POWER OF FLYING POOP

REAL! It's true. Scientists spend time poring over satellite data, trying to find penguin poo. You may be wondering why, and whether your taxpayer dollar is funding these firmament-based fecal finders.

First, it's the British engaging in this activity, according to the CNN article, and second, they do the turd seeking in order to track elusive Emperor penguin colonies in Antarctica. It turns out that the animals themselves are quite camouflaged and impossible to spot by satellites, whereas their caca is not ice-colored at all and relatively easy to pick out.

REAL! If you believe this article in the *New York Post*, a Long Island couple was outside enjoying some sunshine on their deck in 2012 when a plane flew directly overhead and they were splattered with a foul, black liquid.

They believed it was some kind of hydraulic fluid and called the police. It was the helpful policeman who pointed out that it appeared to be "something nastier than that."

FAKE! It is incredibly close, however, to the very real headline of a Fox News story: "The power of flying squirrel poop," which is an investigative report on the Pacific College of Oriental Medicine's claim that flying squirrel feces is a cure for many ailments.

BREAKING NEWS

'Enormous' man hides stolen 32-inch TV in his pants

Man hid snakes, tortoises in his pants, TSA says

Captain America arrested with burrito in his pants

FAKE! To fit 32 inches in his pants, he would *have* to be enormous, wouldn't he?

Slightly less crazy things have happened: in 2012, Fresno's KSEE 24 News ran the headline "Man hides stolen TV in his pants." It seems a police officer thought it was suspicious when a young man "shuffled" his way out of a Walmart and into the parking lot, dropping a box of candy and not stopping to pick it up. The officer called out and the man didn't acknowledge him, so he handcuffed him and found a *19-inch* TV down the front of his pants.

REAL! Imagine trying to look normal in airport security with *seven snakes* and *three tortoises* in your pants. To read West Palm Beach's 2011 WPTV News article, you'd think it must have been the dream of this guy to turn *Snakes on a Plane* into a reality.

REAL! You may assume that Orlando's WFTV was being cheeky when it ran this 2007 headline, but it's actually a pretty faithful description of what happened.

Florida doctor Raymond Adamcik was in great spirits when he decided to embark on a costume-themed pub crawl for medical professionals. But perhaps he had overdone it with the spirits when he allegedly decided to tuck a burrito into his blue tights and walk around asking women to touch it. Certainly he was not thinking like a doctor when he decided to begin groping women when they refused his burrito advances.

The cops were called and this is the very best line from their police report: "There were so many cartoon characters in the bar at the time, all Captain Americas were asked to go outside for a possible identification."

NAKED MAN STEALS
FIRE TRUCK,
KILLS PEDESTRIAN

Late for job, woman
steals fire truck

Teen steals
fire truck, hides it
in the woods

REAL! Chalk that up as an *awful* way to go. It may be funny when a naked man steals a fire truck, but it's not funny at all when he kills someone with it. NBC News had the 2012 story about twenty-two-year-old Kalvin Hunt, who, in his birthday suit, hopped in a fire truck that had just responded to a medical emergency. He managed to hit his victim, as well as several cars and trees, before one tree was big enough to stop him, pinning him in the truck.

Adding insult to injury, Hunt managed to injure three police officers and one EMT *as they tried to rescue him from the truck*. Sheesh.

REAL! Thirty-two-year-old Aurelia Small swiped a fire truck from in front of a dormitory one fine morning in Miami, according to this story from the *Palm Beach Post*. When she was nabbed, her explanation was perfectly rational: she was late for work.

Either she was off her rocker, or she had a very, *very* mean boss.

FAKE! But not far-fetched. There are a few accounts of teenagers stealing fire trucks for joyrides, but none of them so far have been able to keep their quarry.

BURGLAR FOUND NAKED COVERED IN BUTTER, GLITTER

Bloody naked burglar found eating raw chicken

NAKED BURGLAR OVERPOWERED BY NUNS IN CONVENT

FAKE! You get an immediate mental picture though, don't you? I think the Sparkly Butter Bandit would be a great supervillain.

Still, criminals this weird do exist. Utah's KSL TV News ran this headline in 2012: "Burglar found naked covered in chocolate, peanut butter." The delicious thief was believed to have been under the influence of drugs. His grandfather was quoted to say, "Somebody sneaked him something. Maybe bath salts."

REAL! Fox affiliate KDFW ran this article on their website in 2011, describing a Dallas woman's shock at finding a naked man, streaked with blood, chowing down on some raw chicken from her fridge. At least there's an explanation for the blood: he cut himself to ribbons breaking her window and climbing through. As to why he was naked in the first place, or why he was trying to contract salmonella . . . well, that's anybody's guess.

REAL! Nope, it's not the plot to *Sister Act 4*. It really happened! Man, oh man, that would be fun to witness. The story is from a 1965 issue of the *Chicago Tribune*. A nun discovered a nude man prowling through the convent, called her sisters for help, and the women tackled and detained the guy until the police showed up. Brilliant.

MAN COMES BACK TO LIFE AS DOCTORS PREPARE TO REMOVE EYES, KIDNEYS

Killer comes back to life after lethal injection in Oklahoma

BREAKING NEWS

CHINESE WOMAN, 95, CLIMBS OUT OF COFFIN AFTER BEING 'DEAD' FOR DAYS

REAL! You can bet that S. William Winogrond was extremely happy that he didn't wake up an hour after he did. The 1975 story from the *Gettysburg Times* explains that the man had suffered a massive heart attack twelve hours earlier. Winogrond had shown no signs of brain function, and doctors had been keeping his vitals going mechanically. His wife wanted his organs to go to people in need and authorized the surgery.

Winogrond's family had to respond to condolence cards with notes informing friends that he was still alive, and had to cancel the funeral that they had already begun to plan.

If it were I, I'd want to have it anyway. Might as well get to go to your own party.

FAKE! You can sleep easy. The zombie murderer is not on the prowl. This sham headline was inspired by a real *Huffington Post* headline: "Puppy comes back to life after euthanization in Oklahoma." That story is much more heart-warming.

REAL! Not only did Li Xiufeng wake up and climb out of her coffin; she did it after being inside it for *six days*. Thankfully nobody witnessed her emergence, but they did get the joy of finding the coffin open and empty. According to Singapore's English-language *Straits Times*, they found her in the kitchen, making herself something to eat. "I felt so hungry," she was quoted to say.

The nonagenarian Xiufeng had suffered a head injury, and doctors missed her vital signs. She had been kept in an unsealed coffin in her family home in accordance with a Chinese tradition that allows people to come pay their respects.

I wonder how many people had already said goodbye?

Man shot to death for peeing on neighbor's lawn

German man pees, short circuits nightclub

EIGHT MILLION GALLONS OF WATER DRAINED FROM RESERVOIR AFTER MAN URINATES IN IT

FAKE! The real story is much worse. The 2010 *National Post* headline reads "Man shot to death after his dog pees on neighbor's lawn." Retired Illinois truck driver Charles J. Clements represented the "perfect storm" of requirements for such a bizarre crime: he had an obsession with his perfectly manicured lawn, with an award to show for his efforts; he had a dangerously volatile temper; and he had a loaded gun.

A lot of good he's going to be able to do for his lawn from jail.

REAL! Talk about a buzzkill. A clubgoer in Munich may have had problems with the hot spot's owner, says this 2010 Yahoo! News story. That would explain why he dropped trou in the overcrowded nightclub and peed directly onto a set of wall sockets. He caused a short circuit, and the whole place went powerless.

REAL! The 2011 story, from Britain's *Telegraph*, highlights stupidity on two counts. First, it was dumb for twenty-one-year-old Joshua Seater to decide to drunkenly relieve himself in a Portland, Oregon, reservoir. He admitted so publicly: "It was a stupid thing to do. I didn't know it was a water supply, I thought it was a sewage plant."

However, it was *also* stupid for the city to drain the 8 million gallons because of it, costing taxpayers over $35,000 and wasting a lot of water. You may be thinking, "Well, I wouldn't want to drink pee." I hear you, but consider this: there were over a *billion* ounces of clean drinking water in the reservoir, and probably about 8 ounces of pee-pee in Seater's bladder. That means your glass of water would be 128 million parts clean water to 1 part Seater piss. As health scientists pointed out, that's effectively none.

Alton attorney accidentally sues himself

LAWYER SUES HIS OWN FIVE-YEAR-OLD DAUGHTER

KIDNAPPER SUES HOSTAGES, SAYS THEY HAD A DEAL

REAL! The scenario, as depicted by the 2005 article in the Madison/ St. Clair *Record*, is awfully funny. Illinois lawyer Emert Wyss thought he could make some serious money when he invited a woman he was representing to participate in a class action suit against her mortgage lender. As the suit got bigger, he invited four other law firms to get involved.

Poetic justice occurred when, over the course of the suit, it was discovered that the improperly behaved mortgage business was not the one he thought it was. It was actually a different company, which *Wyss himself owned*. He found himself being sued by his own client, and by all four other law firms. Oops.

FAKE! Though lawyers are capable of anything, that would certainly go beyond the pale. Small children do occasionally get sued, such as the 2008 case in which a one- and three-year-old were sued by their mother because the father had passed away without a will. The fortune had passed to the children and left her broke.

Increasingly, minors are the ones doing the suing, such as the 2010 case in which an Arkansas teenager sued his own mom for *harassing him on Facebook.*

REAL! The case of the Topeka kidnapper in this 2011 CBS News article is pretty wacky. On the lam from the police, Jesse Dimmick burst into a couple's home, armed, and offered them an unspecified amount of money in exchange for a hiding spot. He claimed they agreed.

The couple fed Dimmick and watched movies on the couch with him until he fell asleep. Then, like sane people, they snuck out of the house to safety and called the police.

Dimmick filed for $235,000 in damages, claiming they had "a legally binding oral contract."

BREAKING NEWS

90 percent of U.S. money is laced with cocaine

Couple busted for selling cocaine-infused mayonnaise

Student finds cocaine in textbook ordered from Amazon

REAL! If you believe this MSNBC article, and the 2009 study it is based on, there are traces of cocaine in nine out of the ten bills in your wallet right now. The thought is that not *all* of those bills have been directly in contact with the drug, but that some have, and the contact spreads (like a virus) in bank money-counting machines.

FAKE! I was going for the old "That's so strange, it must be true" approach. While cocaine-infused mayo is not a reality, cocaine and mayonnaise have made the news together before. In 1994, a New York City woman opened a sealed jar of Hellmann's that she had bought from the grocery store, and was shocked to discover *thirty-two vials of cocaine inside*.

The mayonnaise giant had no explanation. (I thought maybe she had won a prize or something . . .)

REAL! The 2012 *Huffington Post* article describes college student Sophia Stockton's surprise when she opened the used textbook she ordered from Amazon, and found a bag containing $400 worth of cocaine inside.

She dutifully reported the incident to local police. What makes the story stranger is the subject of the textbook:

Terrorism.

BREAKING NEWS

Fowl! Home run hits stork

STORK HITCHHIKES ON AIRLINER BUT GETS BUM'S RUSH

Millar Derby stork about to be spanked

FAKE! I don't know why there would be a stork at the game, but unfortunate birds have found themselves on the wrong end of a rocketing baseball on a few occasions:

Seagulls interrupted the ball's progress after a base hit in a 2009 major league game, arguably contributing to the Indians's victory against the Royals. In 2003 a Chicago Cubs minor league pitcher faced consequences when he deliberately nailed a roosting osprey during pitching practice. Most shocking was Randy Johnson's 2001 fastball that, in a freak coincidence, struck a dove as it swept across the field. The bird exploded into a cloud of feathers, like something from a cartoon.

REAL! Of course, the 1964 article in the *Youngstown Vindicator* did not assert that an *actual* stork hitchhiked on a plane. Historically, storks have represented the arrival of new babies, and that's the intended meaning here.

A woman went into labor mere moments before her plane was to take off from New York to Chicago. They were able to turn the plane around and rush her to the hospital just in time for her to give birth.

REAL! The 1936 article in St. Petersburg's *Evening Independent* refers to one of the wackiest wills in history. Wealthy lawyer Charles Vance Millar decided to leave his fortune to the Toronto mother who, over a ten-year period, *gives birth to the most babies*. Millar was known to be perversely interested in exploring and exploiting people's greed, and this final experiment is a perfect example.

The "spanking" in question here is the reporter's way of saying that the contest itself was under fire by the government.

In the end, the contest was ruled legal, and four women claimed the inheritance in a tie. They had nine babies each.

CORPULENT COPS FIND
NO JUSTICE IN SCALES

**Conference rejects
"corpulent agenda"**

**America's latest
sports hero is a
corpulent hack**

REAL! The 1972 *Milwaukee Sentinel* story expressed the discomfort and displeasure of several New York City officers who were ordered to go on a diet after being paraded onto a scale. One portly policeman quipped, "If you were in trouble, wouldn't you rather have a beefy cop like me?"

FAKE! Considering the alarmist tones that come along with headlines about America's "obesity epidemic," I wouldn't be surprised if doomsayers started railing about the hidden "corpulent agenda."

This, of course, is a bastardization of the fairly common newspaper headline, "Conference rejects corporate agenda."

REAL! The 2004 headline makes you wonder: how does *Orlando Sentinel* columnist Mike Bianchi *really* feel about golfer John Daly?

THE MAYOR FORBIDS IT

Pick something, anything, and a mayor has tried to stamp it out of his town.

MAYOR BANS LIQUOR; IS BEATEN TO DEATH

Virginia's *Free Lance-Star,* July 10, 1991

It's not fair to say he had it coming, but he might have predicted a backlash. Filiberto Lopez Perez, the mayor of Chanal, Mexico, issued an official decree outlawing liquor. About fifty of the townsfolk expressed their displeasure—by beating Perez *for two hours*, resulting in his death.

MAYOR 'BANS' BARACK OBAMA FROM LAS VEGAS FOR SINS AGAINST THE CITY

London, England's *The Times*, February 20, 2010

Las Vegas mayor Oscar Goodman was never partial to the president, having said of him shortly after the election, "I'm not a fan. I spent three minutes with him at the airport and maybe another five minutes later on. It was enough." But Goodman was particularly angry at Obama's comments that CEOs shouldn't take corporate jets to Vegas during the recession. He declared that the president was hurting the city and that he was officially "banned" from visiting. "I want to assure you that when he comes, I'll do everything I can to give him the boot," he said. A short time later, Obama came to Vegas anyway.

MAYOR FORBIDS WOMEN TO HIDE BEHIND MAKEUP

Chicago Tribune, May 2, 1953

Mayor B. H. Ryan of East Moline, Illinois, claimed he had a rock-solid rationale for banning makeup entirely: he had already proclaimed that all men of the town were to grow beards, and he figured this would only make it fair.

MAYOR STOY FORBIDS FLIRTING, KISSING, SPOONING AND HAND-HOLDING AT ATLANTIC CITY

Baltimore Sun, August 16, 1908

Franklin Pierce Stoy was, by all accounts, a colorful character, alternating between advocating good times in Atlantic City and behaving as the party town's overly strict father. He was arrested multiple times while in office and eventually died in an insane asylum.

MAYOR 'FORBIDS' RAIN ON SATURDAY

Schenectady Gazette, June 12, 1985

Mayor Karen B. Johnson was so excited for that weekend's concert in Schenectady's Central Park that she issued "an executive order forbidding rainfall." She was joking. We hope.

MAYOR FORBIDS RESIDENTS FROM DYING

Australia's *Courier-Mail*, March 14, 2012

The reason Mayor Giulio Cesare Fava gave for his edict is that his town, Falciano del Massico, has no room in the cemetery. He was quoted to say that it is absolutely forbidden for residents "to go beyond the boundaries of earthly life, to go [onto] the afterlife."

MAYOR BANS HAIRY LEGS

Calgary Herald, January 28, 1976

Remind me not to venture to the town of Campo Grande in Brazil because if the law still stands, I'm getting arrested. Mayor Jose Paulo Moura was particularly offended by soccer players, publicly stating, "It is not decent that a group of louts wander around showing off their legs in the middle of a football field, especially those hairy legs." Something tells me Moura had a little secret.

TEACHER TO SERVE 15 DAYS IN TEDDY-BEAR BLASPHEMY CASE

Arctic rescuers save child's teddy bear from ice

HUNDREDS OF TEDDY BEARS BLESSED IN CORPUS CHRISTI

REAL! It's hard to argue that British schoolteacher Gillian Gibbons was doing anything but being selfless and generous when she decided to teach children in Sudan. Unfortunately, ignorance of just how hard a line extreme Muslims can take landed her in hot water, according to this 2007 story on Canada's CBC radio website.

Her crime? Letting her students vote to name the class teddy bear, which she used to teach about animals. The students chose "Muhammad," an extremely common boy's name in the Middle East, and the world over. But because it is also the name of the prophet, a furor erupted, and Gibbons was arrested. She faced a possible *six months in prison and forty lashes*—government officials congratulated themselves on their leniency by reducing the sentence to fifteen days and forced deportation.

FAKE! That would have to be one important stuffed animal. You could, however, find these headlines in 1922: "Teddy Bear escapes ice," and "Arctic rescuers on the Teddy Bear caught in the ice."

Here, "Teddy Bear" is the name a schooner from Nome, Alaska, that became stuck during an Arctic expedition.

REAL! It's fun to picture that particular service, isn't it? Pew after pew of teddy bears in formal wear. The 2011 Associated Press story presents a slightly less silly picture. The teddy bears were rounded up by an organization called the Homicide Survivors Support Group, blessed by South Shore Christian Church in Corpus Christi, Texas, and then distributed to children who have witnessed crimes or lost a family member to homicide.

I give that my blessing as well.

SWEET POTATO LOOKS LIKE ELVIS, SELLS ON EBAY FOR THOUSANDS

George Washington McNugget sells for $8,100 on eBay

BREAKING NEWS

DRIED GLUE THAT KIND OF LOOKS LIKE HOMER SIMPSON SELLING ON EBAY FOR OVER $200K

FAKE! A woman did once try to sell a potato *chip* on eBay that she claimed looked like Elvis, but it received a tepid response.

REAL! Dakota City, Nebraska's Rebekah Speight decided to save a leftover McDonald's McNugget on a whim, according to this 2012 NBC News story, because she thought it looked a bit like George Washington. After keeping it in her freezer for three years, she was participating in a church fundraiser and decided to list it on eBay to see if she got any bites (pardon the pun).

Once the auction ended, she and her church were more than $8,000 richer.

REAL! It's incredibly hard to believe, and yet it's true. This 2012 article from the *Washington Post*'s website lays out the scenario: British gent Christopher Herbert was cleaning out his office closet when he encountered a tiny blob of dried glue. He thought it looked like Homer Simpson (although even he admits that it only looks a *little* like the cartoon character) and decided to list it on eBay "for a bit of a joke."

When the article was written, the winning bid was well over $200,000.

I have a paint chip that looks like Colorado that I plan to list. Easy street, here I come!

Judge orders Florida man to take his wife on a date

JUDGE ORDERS MAN'S LEG AMPUTATED AS PUNISHMENT

Judge orders man to undergo 5 year, gradual castration

REAL! Some call it creative ruling; some call it bench buffoonery. The 2012 NBC News story explains that Joseph Bray was accused of shoving his wife and putting his hands around her throat when she snapped at him for forgetting her birthday. Judge John Hurley decided to hand out a unique punishment: a little romance.

Not only did Hurley order Bray to take his wife on a date but he also specified that it must be dinner at Red Lobster, followed by bowling, and that he must purchase flowers.

Sounds like a good system, right? Bray can throw his wife around all he wants, as long as he takes her out to dinner afterward.

FAKE! That would certainly qualify as cruel and unusual punishment. It was inspired by a 2007 case in which a judge ruled that a South Carolina man could keep his amputated leg after it was accidentally sold at auction. The buyer claimed it was his rightful property, whereas the one-legged man had aspirations of being buried with all his parts.

REAL! The *Boston Globe* reported this bewildering story in 1984. A Kalamazoo, Michigan man was found guilty of sexually assaulting his underage stepdaughter over a period of seven years, until she ran away. Rather than serve jail time, the judge ordered that he undergo "chemical castration," a drug therapy that would diminish his sex drive completely.

The craziest part is this: the drug was manufactured by the Upjohn pharmaceutical company, which was founded by the grandfather of the accused, making him the *heir to the fortune*. He'd go on to get rich off the company, but not before being forced to sample his own products.

DEFRIENDING WOMAN ON FACEBOOK LEADS TO DOUBLE MURDER

Man arrested for writing "I love you to death" on friend's Facebook wall

HUSBAND HACKED WIFE TO DEATH WITH MEAT CLEAVER AFTER SHE CHANGED FACEBOOK STATUS TO SINGLE

REAL! In the most awful case of overreaction ever, a young Nashville, Tennessee, couple was brutally murdered after they "defriended" a girl on Facebook, according to this article run in 2012 by the *Christian Post*.

It was the girl's father who decided to exact retribution for the snub. He went to the couple's house, shot them both, and slit the husband's throat for good measure. In an appalling testament to the senseless savagery of the crime, the killer left the couple's crying eight-month-old baby in her dead mother's arms.

FAKE! Nevertheless, people are arrested for Facebook comments all the time. Any threat of violence, even as a joke, can lead to officers knocking on your door. Outside the United States, several people have been arrested, and punished, for simply criticizing the government on the site. One Tennessee woman was even arrested for simply "poking" someone else on Facebook (because it violated a restraining order).

REAL! Britain's *Daily Mail* really doesn't hold back on the headlines.

In this 2008 article, London truck driver Wayne Forrester had a contentious, on-again, off-again relationship with his wife Emma, said mutual friends. When she finally gave him the boot, she sealed the deal by changing her Facebook relationship status to "single," and posting that she was looking for companionship.

Forrester described his reaction as a "blur" and said that it was as though he were watching someone else do it. He loaded up on alcohol and cocaine before driving over to her house and murdering her in her bed with a meat cleaver.

Forrester went to jail for "life," but lawyers pointed out that he could be on the streets again in as little as fourteen years.

Mountain lions prowl about the streets of Salt Lake City

WHITE WOMEN PROWL MANILA STREETS

EXOTIC ANIMALS PROWL OHIO, SCHOOLS CLOSED

REAL! This delicious headline is well over a hundred years old, having appeared in the *Newburgh Daily Journal* in 1894.

Heavy snows that year had driven all kinds of wild animals down from the mountains and into the streets of Salt Lake City, which at the time had a population of 65,000.

FAKE! Look out! The real headline from the *Manila Bulletin* is "'White Ladies' to prowl streets," referring to white-uniformed traffic cops. The 2010 article does get a little weird, though: "The deployment of these mostly attractive traffic enforcers is one of the few innovations being introduced . . . "

I take it that it's somehow important that the ladies be "mostly attractive"? It goes on to say that the "lady enforcers will be ably backed up by male counterparts."

Oh, that's a relief.

REAL! It sounds preposterous, but it really happened in 2011, as the CNN article attests.

Sheriff's deputies drove around eastern Ohio armed with shotguns and night vision goggles, hoping to hunt down the "bears, lions, tigers, cheetahs, wolves, giraffes and camels" that were on the loose. The owner of the farm on which they lived had decided to release them, and then take his own life. Unfortunately, his selfishness affected the animals as well, because officers were forced to shoot and kill nearly fifty of them, including several endangered ones. A handful were able to be rescued and delivered to the local zoo.

BREAKING NEWS

Man robs bank to pay for boob job

Toothless woman robs bank for denture money

Man robs bank to pay his own defense lawyers

REAL! If you believe this 2007 article in the United Kingdom's *Metro* newspaper, not only did Austrian man Robert Steinwirt rob a bank to buy fake boobs; the operation was to be for his *transvestite lover*. I wonder if he got the idea from the Al Pacino movie *Dog Day Afternoon*?

The plastic surgeon who was to perform the operation was suspicious of the way Steinwirt wanted to pay immediately, up front, and in cash. He called the police, and the Austrian was *busted* before his lover could be. Get it? Wow, that's a terrible pun.

REAL! Pennsylvania woman Evelyn Marie Fuller was frustrated that welfare wouldn't cover her dentures right away and decided to take matters into her own hands, according to this 2012 NBC Philadelphia article. She passed a note through the bank window, demanding a specific amount of cash. Unfortunately for her, toothlessness is a fairly memorable trait, and one of the other bank tellers recognized her from church.

She was arrested on two counts of robbery, one of theft, and one of making a terrorist threat.

FAKE! It would be ironic, wouldn't it? There have been a couple of cases of people stealing to pay their legal bills, and even a couple of cases of *bank-robbing lawyers*, but nobody has robbed a bank solely to pay their lawyer. Yet.

WIFE ON TRIAL AFTER HUSBAND'S PENIS-FIRE DEATH

Greek woman sets fire to British tourist's genitals

Man critically injured in Grand Crossing testicle fire

REAL! According to this riveting news.com.au story, Rajini Narayan saw her husband hug another woman in 2008, decided he must be having an affair, and subsequently set his junk on fire as he slept.

Unfortunately for the Australian and her husband, the alcohol she used made the fire difficult to put out. To make things worse, he leaped out of bed and flailed about, which is understandable, but in the process he knocked over the bottle of alcohol, spreading the fire into the house and the house next door. As if it couldn't get any worse, it did. After a few days in the hospital, her husband was unable to combat the infections, and he died.

REAL! If things really went down the way this 2009 News Limited story suggests, it's a case of poetic justice. The unidentified woman claims to have been minding her own business at the bar when a drunken British tourist groped her between her legs. She says she turned around, and he had his naughty bits out for her to see. Thinking quickly, she splashed him with her glass of sambuca.

This is where accounts begin to differ. The man claims that she then flicked her lighter and set his undercarriage on fire. She claims that she turned back around and that he must have set himself alight when trying to light a cigarette.

Either way, fellow citizens of Crete rallied in support of the woman, publicly declaring her a "hero."

FAKE! It's believable that such a fire would result in critical injuries. The headline was lifted from the *Chicago Sun-Times*, with the word "vehicle" replacing the word "testicle."

Vehicle fires are much more common, though I would say both could seriously affect traffic.

SAN FRANCISCO SURGEON REPLACES MECHANICAL MAN'S SEVERED HAND WITH FLAMETHROWER

Scientist becomes world's first cyborg

HALF-MAN, HALF-MACHINE TO CLEAN UP CITY

FAKE! Flame-shooting cyborgs may haunt my dreams, but they're not around yet. The headline was inspired by this real-life *San Francisco Chronicle* one: "SF surgeon replaces mechanic's severed thumb with toe."

Ah, much better.

REAL! There are plenty of academics that would be thrilled to engage you in a debate as to what constitutes a "cyborg." Some say the term, which means "part-human, part-robot" is loose enough to count people with pacemakers as cyborgs.

Others, like this *Guardian* article, think it happened when University of Reading professor Kevin Warwick had a robotic, computerized, metal shaft surgically implanted in his arm. Wires run from the device to the surface of his skin near the elbow, so that he can plug himself in and download data. One hope was that the device would be able to give him a *sixth sense*—the ability to sense the space around him like a bat.

REAL! I get it that automated, side-loading garbage trucks had not been seen before in California when this 1988 headline appeared in the *Modesto Bee*, but to alarmingly top the metro section with the assertion that "half-man, half-machine" is going to "clean up the city" seems a bit like overkill.

Personally, I think the editor had been waiting to run something like that since *Robocop* came out in 1984.

MODEL SAYS HUGE BREASTS SAVED HER LIFE IN CAR CRASH

Breast implants save Israeli's life in rocket attack

BREAKING NEWS

RHINOCEROS CHARGES REPORTER; BIG BOOBS 'SAVED HER LIFE'

REAL! While model Sheyla Hershey knew she could make money with her enormous chest (she is the former record holder for the world's largest fake breasts), she probably didn't know that they could save her life.

The 2012 NBC Philadelphia story explains that Hershey got into a car accident, and her car's airbags failed to deploy. It's a good thing she was equipped with two of her own! She insists that her *38KKK* bust is the only reason she's alive today.

REAL! The *New Zealand Herald* ran this 2006 story about a Hezbollah rocket attack that smashed through a building in Jerusalem, sending a twenty-four-year-old Israeli woman flying. She was rushed to Nahariya Hospital where doctors found pieces of shrapnel lodged in her breasts, just inches from her heart.

A hospital spokesman said, in no uncertain terms, that the woman's implants saved her life.

FAKE! Okay, so breast implants might not have saved a woman from a *rhinoceros*, but we've proven they've saved women from shrapnel and car crash–related blunt force trauma.

There are many more examples of implants saving lives, including a Russian woman whose fake boobs stopped her husband's *knife* attack from reaching her heart, and multiple stories of implants *stopping bullets*, including a case that involved an automatic weapon at short range.

Clearly, insurance providers should start to cover breast implants. You know, for safety.

Pokie pushers make picky pacers

PRETTY PICKLES PLEASE PALATES, PACKERS PLEAD

Picker pickers can dicker with thicker picker pack

FAKE! It's an amalgamation of two real headlines: "Pokie push-ers inspired by greed," from the *Sydney Morning Herald*, and "picky Pacers," from the *Indianapolis Star*. "Pokie pushers" are people who provide poker machines to hungry gamblers, and "picky Pacers" were the Indiana Pacers when they were being choosy about their roster.

REAL! The playful 1929 *St. Petersburg Times* article told of an amazing new development in the snack food industry: "shapely" pickles. The article quoted professor George E. Starr of the Univer-sity of Michigan, who said, "Civilized Americans demand that their food be pleasing to the eye as well as to the palate, and at last have grown a cucumber that we believe will answer both requirements."

Well said, sir!

REAL! This tongue twister is the lead line of a 1965 *Vancouver Sun* article about berry farmers. A sudden change in weather had ripened berries prematurely, and berry farmers made a call for workers to come and harvest. They chose from the pool of people that showed up, making them "picker pickers," and sometimes fought over work-ers, meaning that they "dickered." They also marveled at the sheer number of interested persons who answered the ad—the "thicker picker pack."

BREAKING NEWS

Minneapolis will pay $165,000 to zombies

Michigan State University offers zombie survival class

Japanese-Canadians feel zombie will resolve dispute quickly

REAL! If the writer of the 2010 Minneapolis *Star Tribune* story knew that the headline was a little bit misleading, he didn't let on.

It refers to a settlement the city made to seven people who had been wrongfully arrested while performing "street theater," which involved dressing up like zombies and shuffling around downtown. Still, the article referred to the protesters as "zombies" throughout.

Wait . . . maybe they really *are* zombies?!

REAL! The 2012 NBC News article gives the details of the totally legit U of M class, "Surviving the Coming Zombie Apocalypse: Catastrophes & Human Behavior." Many bitchers and moaners have complained that the class is yet another example of ridiculous, hippie, liberal arts brainwashing and a waste of taxpayer dollars, but the class is really an example of excellent marketing.

Professor Glen Stutzky pointed out that the class uses zombie invasion as a metaphor to teach students about how people behave in times of crisis. Students study pandemics such as the bubonic plague and "learn about the nature, scope and impact of catastrophic events on individuals, families, societies, civilizations and the Earth itself."

Fun!

FAKE! While a zombie may very well resolve a dispute quickly, this headline is inaccurate. The real one from a 1986 article in the *Ottowa Citizen* goes a little something like this: "Japanese-Canadians feel Crombie will resolve dispute quickly." It's about providing wartime reparations and is *far* more boring than an article about zombies would be.

PRUDE VIEWED NUDES, SUES, CUES FEUD

Nothing rude in nude if mood isn't lewd

No nudes is good nudes

FAKE! I tried to channel my inner Dr. Seuss when I made that headline up from scratch. I can think of a couple of real-life situations that could have been written up with that title, however.

REAL! Speaking of Dr. Seuss, the writer of this 1963 column in the *Hartford Courant* had exceeded his recommended daily allowance of whimsy when he came up with this one. It was a playful account of the arrest of a photographer and his subject when they were encountered shooting naked photos in public. The subtitle said it all: "Depending on how the law's construed, there's nothing rude about a proper nude, as long as her mood skirts the lewd."

REAL! The front-page item of a June 1991 *New York Post* referred to a monumental decision by the Supreme Court. The high court voted, 5–4, to give communities the power to ban nudity at strip clubs.

Critics proclaimed that the decision constituted an attack on Americans's freedom of expression, but the conservative judges declared that the public's "moral disapproval" outweighed that right.

I SEE JESUS . . .

I grew up in the era of Elvis sightings, and though he's dead and gone, he was "spotted" at gas stations and national parks, and his image was seen on a piece of toast and in a ghostly photograph. But when it comes to surprise appearances, the King has nothing on the Messiah. Here's a small sample of ridiculous Jesus sightings that for some reason made the news.

WOMAN SEES FACE OF JESUS IN SOCK

The Telegraph, December 28, 2011

She was devastated when she moved the sock from the clothesline and Jesus vanished.

METHUEN WOMAN SEES JESUS ON BOTTOM OF HER CLOTHES IRON

Boston Globe, November 27, 2009

A brilliant excuse to get out of housework.

SC COUPLE SEES JESUS ON WAL-MART RECEIPT

Georgia's WJBF News,
July 19, 2011

They say that one day Jesus Christ will return . . . the Shake Weight you bought him.

JESUS APPEARS ON GOOGLE MAPS

Metro, April 27, 2010

It's a field in Hungary that, from a great distance, I admit looks a lot like Jesus.

MAN SEES JESUS IN TORTILLA

Ohio's WNWO News,
March 2, 2012

The image appeared in David Sandoval's tortilla as he was sitting down to dinner on Ash Wednesday . . . cue *Twilight Zone* music . . .

STUDENT SEES FACE OF JESUS IN FRYING PAN

Rutherglen Reformer,
March 12, 2010

He fell asleep while cooking and woke up to a smoke-filled room. He grabbed the frying pan off the stove and was confronted with the image. He maintains Jesus saved him from perishing in a house fire.

WOMAN SEES IMAGE OF JESUS IN POWER METER

Tampa's WTSP News, March 22, 2012

A woman was praying outside of her trailer home in the Torchlite RV Park in Clermont, Florida, when she noticed Jesus's face in the smudges on a power meter. And then it made the news.

WOMAN SAYS JESUS APPEARS IN SON'S MELTED CRAYONS

Detroit's WXYZ News, December 19, 2011

I know somebody who's got some "melted crayons," and it's not her son.

JESUS 'APPEARED IN MY CHEWING GUM'

The Telegraph, April 6, 2010

Do you think she spit it out after each chew to look at it until she got it right?

CANCER PATIENT SEES JESUS IN MRI RESULTS

NBC News, October 5, 2010

The poor woman was contradicted by some religious groups, who claimed the image was actually of *Satan*.

JESUS SEEN IN CHICKEN'S FEATHERS

Metro, July 23, 2010

It's starting to be clear that Jesus really gets around.

JESUS IMAGE APPEARS ON DOG

Metro, July 6, 2011

The craziest part is that the likeness appeared on the dog's *butt*. Seriously.

But the award for the best "I SEE JESUS" headline goes to the *Daily Mail* for this July 1, 2010, headline:

FACE OF JESUS ON DRAINPIPE: IT'S THE SECOND PLUMBING

ROGUE MICKEY MOUSE CAUSES HIGH ALERT AT OHIO SCHOOL

Mickey Mouse hunted in Atlantic

MICKEY MOUSE MUST DIE, SAYS SAUDI ARABIAN CLERIC

REAL! It's true. As this article in the *Mumbai Mirror* states, an Ohio school went into emergency-mode lockdown in 2012 when Mickey Mouse was spotted on campus.

A well-meaning mom dressed up as Mickey Mouse to surprise her daughter's class. She was properly signed in, but when she went to the bathroom and changed, campus security thought Mickey Mouse was potentially roaming the halls looking for children to prey on.

Eventually the miscommunication was cleared up, and the students were free to go about their day, unmolested by giant rodents.

FAKE! In 1958, the Air Force and the Navy were indeed searching the Atlantic for a mouse. It was not, however, Mickey Mouse. It was Wickie, the Space Mouse.

See, the government at the time was in the habit of launching rockets into space with a live mouse. Their goal was to recover the nose of each rocket after reentry and see if the mouse was still alive. The *Pittsburgh Press* ran the real headline: "Space mouse hunted in Atlantic."

Data showed that Wickie survived the journey back to Earth, but the nose cone containing her was never found.

REAL! In 2008, Saudi cleric Muhammad Munajid pointed out that according to Islamic law, all mice are "Satan's soldiers" and must be killed, whether they are flesh-and-blood or paint-and-pixel.

The *Telegraph* article quoted Munajid: "Creatures that are repulsive by nature, by logic, and according to Islamic law have become wonderful and are loved by children. Even mice. . . according to Islamic law, Mickey Mouse should be killed in all cases."

He went on to point out that "Tom and Jerry" are Satanic as well.

ABANDONED TODDLER SURVIVES ON MOSS, GRASS, ANTS

Toddler survives on potato chips, toilet water

BREAKING NEWS

TODDLER SURVIVES 2 ½ WEEKS ALONE ON KETCHUP, DRY PASTA

FAKE! Thank heavens. But it was inspired by this delightful headline of a 1983 issue of Meriden, Connecticut's *Record-Journal*: "'Dumb' marine survives on moss, grass, ants."

It was the story of Lance Corporal Karl Bell, who was lost in the Sierra wilderness for more than five weeks after falling into a ravine and breaking his ankle. Bell described himself to reporters as "dumb" for getting lost, which led the editors to phrase the headline in this somewhat cruel way.

REAL! The only bright spot to this utterly horrible account in a 1987 copy of the *Pittsburg Post-Gazette* is that the seventeen-month-old Kansas City girl survived.

Police believe that her father shot and killed her mother, then turned the gun on himself, leaving the toddler, her three-month-old sister, and the family dog to fend for themselves. The girl just wasn't old enough to understand what to do. It's thought that she learned to drink toilet water from the dog and that potato chips were the only edible thing within reach. She survived for *three weeks* this way. Her infant sister, strapped into a baby seat in the living room, was not so lucky.

REAL! In this 2003 story in Florida's *Lakeland Ledger*, a woman was arrested and didn't tell police that her daughter was home alone. The mother also told the girl's father (from whom she was separated) that the girl was staying with neighbors.

When the dad had no luck knocking on neighbors' doors, he convinced the building manager to open up the apartment. He discovered his daughter watching cartoons, covered in dried ketchup. She made a full recovery.

The mother got slapped with an additional charge: child abuse.

Overworked bimbo found to be psychotic

HERE COMES ANOTHER BIMBO ERUPTION

V-D Day! Paris liberated, bimbos rejoice

FAKE! Though it *could* be real, and with multiple meanings. Searching through archives, you would find the following headlines: "Bimbo won't entertain folks" in the *Portsmouth Times*, "Bimbo was psychotic" in the *Evening Independent*, and most revealingly, "Too much training: Bimbo the whale psychotic, retires" in the *Free Lance-Star*, all of them from 1965.

That's right. Bimbo was a 4,500-pound whale, and he was found to be psychotic.

REAL! During Clinton's long road to the presidency, former deputy chair of his campaign Betsey Wright coined the phrase "bimbo eruption" to describe the steady stream of women popping up and claiming to have had affairs with him. She may have been trying to deflect blame from Bill and categorize the women as opportunists, but the media and opponents loved the phrase, and it came back to haunt him.

This 1994 *Denver Post* column found delight in detailing the next woman up to bat, Paula Jones, as she went ahead with a sexual harassment lawsuit against the president.

To this day, politicians and the media use the phrase "bimbo eruption" to refer to any case of women publicly declaring sexual relationships with political figures.

REAL! The ever classy *New York Post* let the world know just what it thinks of Paris Hilton in this front-page headline from 2007. The iconic Hilton heiress had just been released from jail (hence, "Paris liberated").

Florida man accused of sandwich assault

CAMBRIDGE STUDENT ARRESTED FOR JELLY ATTACK

TEEN GETS JAIL TIME FOR PEANUT BUTTER ASSAULT

REAL! It's a true story, even though "sandwich assault" isn't a legitimate, on-the-books crime. Instead, nineteen-year-old Emmanuelle Rodriguez was charged with domestic battery when he decided to attack his girlfriend with a sandwich, according to this 2008 article on Albuquerque's KOAT News website.

While being struck in the face repeatedly by a sandwich would certainly not be pleasant, it doesn't sound that dangerous. Unless the victim is *driving a car* at the time, which Rodriguez's girlfriend was indeed doing, with their seven-month-old baby in the back.

FAKE! But it *could* be real. In 2008, Cambridge student Nadia Witkowski was celebrating graduation by participating in a girl-on-girl jelly wrestling contest. According to media reports, she won the match but was booed because the other woman was prettier. She then decided to march into the crowd and attack. One female onlooker's nose was broken, and Witkowski was arrested.

REAL! Boise's KBOI News explains that Wenatchee, Washington's Joshua Hickson grabbed a friend's peanut butter sandwich and wiped it on a classmate's forehead (sounds like most of my days in the middle school lunchroom). Hickson was arrested, charged with assault, and sentenced to jail time.

Overkill, you say? Not so, says the judge, who determined that Hickson knew his fellow student was extremely allergic to peanuts. You could argue that it was assault with a deadly, delicious weapon.

ARRESTED PERFORMANCE ARTIST STRIPPED NAKED, COVERED SELF IN WHALE BLUBBER

Naked man is found dead on whale's back in SeaWorld pool

ARCTIC BELUGAS TAMED BY NAKED SWIMMING RUSSIAN SCIENTIST

FAKE! I'm surprised how easy it was for me to dream up such a ridiculous image.

REAL! The good news is that the Florida man who hid in the park until after closing time got to realize his dream of swimming with a killer whale. The bad news is that the killer whale lived up to its name.

Since the *Los Angeles Times* reported this story in 1999, the Orlando whale struck again. In 2010 the five-ton Tilikum (who is the largest orca in captivity) pulled trainer Dawn Brancheau into the water, snapped her spine, and held her until long after she had drowned.

Tilikum still "performs" at SeaWorld Orlando.

REAL! Scientist and diver Natalia Avseenko is not a pervert—she swims with beluga whales in the buff for completely scientific reasons, says the *Huffington Post*. Apparently, belugas don't respond well to the touch of synthetic materials, and scientists believe that nude humans are much more likely to pacify the huge beasts.

You gotta give credit to Avseenko. She swims with potentially dangerous, 3,000-pound, wild animals in *30°F water* while holding her breath for *ten minutes at a time* without a stitch on her.

What have you done today?

BREAKING NEWS

Man keeps boa warm in boxers

Police: stolen rolls of pennies found in woman's panties

Pickled pig's foot, nibbled sausage found in Vero man's undies

REAL! Ohio cops had a bit of a shock after they arrested Brian Dawson in 1995 for driving without a license, says Dubuque, Iowa's *Telegraph-Herald*. While Dawson was changing into his new prison uniform, a boa constrictor "popped out of his underwear." Dawson claimed he kept the snake in his boxers so that it could keep warm.

The best part: the boa turned out to be stolen, and was reunited with its owner.

FAKE! If a man can hide a snake in his boxer shorts, then a woman could hide pennies in her panties.

REAL! It must have been a slow news day when ABC News ran this headline in 2011.

A hungry and homeless Vero Beach, Florida, man wandered into a Chevron, grabbed various meats, and shoved them into his dirty underwear. He also swiped a twenty-four-ounce Yuengling beer and put it in his back pocket.

The article went on to explain what "pickling" is, and that pickled pig's feet are "the classic Southern snack." It did not include, though, the rich Southern tradition of marinating pig's feet and sausage in a homeless man's soiled drawers, which gives them an extra zip.

BELLINGHAM MAN CUTS OFF OWN ARM WITH GUILLOTINE

Sleep walker cuts off own arm with ax

Frenchman cuts off own arm, tries to flush it down the toilet

REAL! There's really not much more to this story, reported in 2011 by Seattle's NWCN News. A Bellingham, Washington, man walked into a medical clinic with just one arm. Later, police went to his campsite where they found "a homemade guillotine and the man's right arm."

Nobody's quite sure what possessed him.

REAL! The 1933 article in the *Milwaukee Journal* claimed "20 year old farm youth" Stanley Benson rose from his bed in the dead of night, walked about in his sleep, then went to the wood pile and chopped off his own arm with an axe.

Benson had no recollection of or explanation for cutting off his arm.

FAKE! That's crazy. But it was inspired by this real 2012 headline from French public radio station RFI's website: "French man cuts off rival's penis and flushes it down toilet." The "rival" was a man who came over to tell the attacker that he'd been having an affair with his wife of fourteen years and the mother of his children. He didn't get the response that he'd hoped for, I take it.

SKATEBOARDING TEENS SUBDUE RAVING, BELLIGERENT SECURITY GUARD

Belligerent flight attendant subdued by passengers

BREAKING NEWS

RUNS AMUCK WITH HIS CLUB; A BELLIGERENT SPECIAL POLICEMAN SUBDUED BY A MINISTER

FAKE! That's ridiculous. We all know it's security guards' jobs to beat on skateboarding punks, not the other way around.

REAL! We constantly hear stories of flight attendants having to deal with rowdy passengers, but this was the first time I'd heard of such a role reversal. Fresno's KSEE News ran the story in 2012 and described the way a harried American Airlines flight attendant went off on a bone-chilling rant over the PA system while the plane taxied for takeoff, including announcing that the plane would crash and everyone would die.

The woman is thought to have been dealing with stress due to 9/11 and America's bankruptcy, and it's believed she had gone off of her prescribed psychiatric medicine.

Not surprisingly, many people on the plane elected not to fly that day.

REAL! This great little time capsule is from an August 1900 article in the *New York Times*. A Harlem policeman, John Horan, was said to have started ranting and dashing about, whacking innocent people with his billy club. Thank God that a physically fit minister came along and got the officer under control. In court, it was revealed that he was thoroughly drunk at the time, a condition that he blamed on his wife.

Man steals glacier for designer ice cubes

MAN STEALS FISH TANK, GOES ON RAMPAGE

Bold man steals Taft's opossum

REAL! Chile's Jorge Montt glacier, a thousand miles south of Santiago, is considered a national monument and is melting at a rate of half a mile per year. That's why officials were surprised when they discovered that a man had been severing huge chunks of the iceberg, whittling it into "designer" ice cubes, and selling them to fancy folks who want an expensive and luxury-minded way to cool their drinks. The 2012 ABC News story pointed out that as the Jorge Montt glacier melts, it makes a "popping noise" and releases air that has been trapped for hundreds or thousands of years.

FAKE! The headline makes a lot more sense when you subtract a word and render it in its correct form: "Man steals tank, goes on rampage." The 1995 *Chicago Tribune* story detailed how a guy managed to sneak into a National Guard armory and drive a tank out, smashing all sorts of things before he hit a highway divider and was shot and killed by police.

REAL! The subtitle of the article from a 1909 *Chicago Tribune* was "Sweet potatoes which formed remainder of dinner also purloined." Our portly 27th president was fond of eating possum, but on that particular night, he was denied. The crook was bold indeed to sneak past hordes of Dallas police and multiple Secret Service men, get into Taft's train car, and swipe the president's dinner.

CUTS OFF LEG . . .

We all have that friend who is constantly losing things. His keys, his wallet, his homework . . . but, of all the things a person *could* lose, you'd think a leg would be the hardest. And yet, throughout history, people have managed to do it.

FATHER ACCIDENTALLY CUTS OFF DAUGHTER'S LEG

Chicago Tribune, June 26, 1921

How Evansville, Indiana, farmer John Dye managed to run his daughter "accidentally" through a sugar cane–cutting machine is lost to the mists of time. We only know that it happened.

WOMAN CALMLY CUTS OFF LEG

St. Petersburg Times,
August 12, 1942

There are hundreds of counts of people cutting off an appendage after an accident, but the fact that this woman did it "calmly" is what's so unsettling. A fisherwoman's foot became entangled in a boat engine, so as she and an onlooker attested, she removed her foot with a serrated fishing knife in a perfectly peaceful manner.

DOCTOR CUTS OFF WRONG LEG OF ENGLISH WIDOW

Milwaukee Journal,
February 13, 1968

The elderly lady needed one leg amputated, but the surgeon accidentally removed the other. She wound up legless. The saintly woman said, "We all make mistakes. I won't have a word said against him."

MAN PLANS CUTTING HIS LEGS OFF ONLINE

ABC News, August 14, 2001

Partially paralyzed man Paul Morgan planned to cut off his own legs at home in protest because insurance wouldn't pay for him to get a legitimate operation. He set up a website and told visitors it would be $20 a pop to watch. He never went through with it.

TRAIN CUTS OFF MAN'S LEG; TRAIN CUTS OFF BABY'S LEGS; FOOT CAUGHT IN FROG, TRAIN CUTS OFF LEG; MAN QUIETLY WATCHES TRAIN CUT OFF HIS LEG . . .

Boston Daily Globe, **April 5, 1916;** *Sydney Morning Herald,* **November 29, 1952;** *Hartford Courant,* **December 9, 1916;** *Meriden Record,* **August 2, 1935**

There are a hundred more like this.

TRAIN LOPS OFF LEGS, RESCUER FAINTS, DIES

Regina, Canada's *Leader-Post,* **August 8, 1956**

Not only did a man lose his legs, but a firefighter who tried to rescue him went into shock, had a heart attack, and died. Talk about a double whammy.

TRAIN CUTS OFF MAN'S OTHER LEG

Wilmington, North Carolina's *Star-News,* **May 19, 1994**

That's right. An Alabama man got drunk, passed out on railroad tracks, and lost a second leg when a train came by, after losing his first *the exact same way eight years earlier*.

TRAIN CUTS OFF HIS LEG; BUT IT WAS A WOODEN ONE

Indiana's *Warsaw Union,* **May 7, 1930**

At least not all train-amputation stories end in pain and misery. The story describes onlookers' abject horror when they witnessed a Mississippi boy's fall underneath a freight train. His leg was clearly mangled, but the boy was smiling. Turns out it didn't hurt, and was thoroughly replaceable.

Stoned dad leaves baby in oven, police say

POLICE: STONER DAD PACKED TWO JOINTS, BEER, CANDY IN TODDLER'S LUNCHBOX

Stoned dad stones daughters to death

REAL! It's okay to laugh because the baby was fine. Los Angeles's KTLA News reported the 2010 story of Kentucky's Larry Long, who allegedly drank a fifth of whiskey, got high on marijuana, and decided to put his baby in the oven. The baby's mom, who was asleep at the time, woke up several hours later to sounds of crying and found her infant in the unlikeliest of places.

Thankfully, Long never turned the oven on—making it just a really, really uncomfortable crib. Long claimed he had been hallucinating.

FAKE! The real story is, happily, not nearly as awful. The *Inquisitor* ran this headline in 2011: "Stoner dad drops joint in toddler's lunchbox, gets arrested." The fumbling father dropped the marijuana cigarette into his eighteen-month-old kid's lunchbox accidentally, making for a funny surprise when staff at the day care found it. They called the police, the Connecticut man's house was searched, and a small amount of cannabis and paraphernalia were found.

He was charged with possession and "impairing the morals of a child."

REAL! There's really nothing funny about this one. As reported in the *Himalayan Times*, a Nepalese man named Bhakta Bahadur Rumba became thoroughly inebriated in 2012 and decided to pick up a boulder and use it to crush his three young daughters, one after the other.

Luckily his wife and son were away at a wedding party, and were spared his wrath.

Woman calls ex-boyfriend 65,000 times

WOMAN CALLS 6 SELVES TO TESTIFY IN ASSAULT TRIAL

Woman calls pet rat 'husband'

REAL! A Dutch woman was charged with stalking, according to this 2011 AOL News story, when it was revealed that she had called a man 65,000 times in *one year*. That roughly works out to a call every eight minutes, night and day, for an entire year. If you assume that she slept at least six hours a night, then she was calling him every six minutes, every day, during waking hours.

Hilariously, the woman claimed she was in a relationship with the man and the calls weren't excessive. The man denied any relationship.

REAL! The *Toledo Blade* reported this intriguing 1990 story about a Wisconsin woman with multiple personality disorder. She charged a man with sexually assaulting her in a public park, while he claimed it was consensual.

The law says that sexual contact can't be legal if one partner suffers from a disability that makes them "incapable of appraising a person's conduct." The woman, who doctors said had forty-six distinct personalities, summoned six of them to testify in the trial. During the three-hour "eerie" testimony, she would frequently close her eyes, bow her head, and suddenly pop to life in a completely new personality.

FAKE! Disturbing? Yes. True? No. The inspiration came from a 1984 issue of Ohio's *Daily Times*: "Woman calls pet rat hero." Aww!

Vicky Downey had been sound asleep when she was awakened by her pet rat, Yentl, licking her face. She immediately saw that her bedroom was filling with smoke, and her electric blanket and mattress were starting to smolder. She dashed out of bed, and moments later, the mattress was engulfed in flames.

Rodents are typically hardwired to flee from smoke and fire, making Yentl's actions particularly fascinating.

Police use stun gun on 6-year-old

CHICAGO POLICE TASER 102-YEAR-OLD WOMAN

NAKED MAN TASERED 'IN THE ASS'

REAL! The 2004 incident, as captured by this *Pittsburgh Tribune-Review* headline, caused a national uproar, as you can guess.

We can give the officers credit as far as they found themselves in a shocking situation: the boy they encountered was clutching a piece of broken glass, waving it around, and gouging himself with it. However, we can all agree that two adult cops could probably have taken control of a six-year-old in a more graceful way.

The boy made a full physical recovery and was submitted to psychiatric evaluation.

FAKE! You have to give Chicago cops more credit than that. They know a 102-year-old would be way too old to be a candidate for getting tasered. In your eighties, however? Look out. The *Digital Journal* ran the accurate headline: "Chicago police taser 82-year-old woman."

Officers claimed the woman was swinging a hammer at them and they were left with no choice. The woman's daughter claimed she had dementia and that, being an old lady, she should have been relatively easy for two able-bodied cops to subdue.

REAL! You can generally count on Britain's *Metro* newspaper to let it all hang out when it comes to their headlines. Speaking of letting it all hang out, that's precisely what a St. Louis man decided to do at a 2007 Girl Talk concert, for which he was summarily electrocuted by area police.

The *Metro* retelling quoted a female witness: "He was tased in the ass for a prolonged period of time. It was terrible."

BREAKING NEWS

*Pudding saves lives,
one at least*

Ice cream saves
youngster's life

Candy saves child's
life in spanking case

REAL! North Carolina's K104.7 news website ran this misleading headline in 2012. The "Pudding" in question is, in fact, a fat tabby cat. The story behind Pudding is fantastic.

Wisconsin woman Amy Jung went to a shelter with her son to play with the cats. She and Pudding had a special bond, and she made the impulse decision to take him home. That night, Jung had a seizure in bed. Pudding sat on her chest, batting her face and biting her nose until she revived. She was too weak to call out or reach the phone. Pudding *woke up her son*, and he called 911.

You could say that Jung saved Pudding's life by adopting him, and that Pudding immediately returned the favor.

REAL! According to a 1961 copy of the *Saskatoon Star-Phoenix*, British Columbia's three-year-old Diana Friesan blithely ingested a few gulps of gasoline. Medics on the scene claimed that the dish of ice cream she had eaten just before provided her with a "protective lining" that insulated her from poisoning long enough for them to save her life.

FAKE! This sham headline was inspired by a real one in which candy was the culprit, not the savior. In 1926, the *Milwaukee Sentinel* ran this headline: "Candy perils child's life; spanking effective 'cure.'"

It turns out that a two-year-old Weehawken, New Jersey, boy began to choke after swallowing an entire lollipop, stick and all. The article reports that "a good old fashioned spanking, administered by a nurse" dislodged the lolly and saved the boy's life once and for all.

DAVID BOWIE BLINDED BY LOLLIPOP

First-graders beat up lollipop man, 73

Heroin lollipops seized from sweaty Guatemalan at airport

REAL! The lead line of this 2004 story from XFM London's website is just a little bit deceptive. David Bowie is not, in fact, blind. He did, however, risk losing sight in one eye when a stupid fan launched his lollipop at him during a concert in Oslo.

The lolly hit Bowie stick-first, in that sweet spot between eyeball and eyelid. The singer called his attacker a "coward" and canceled the rest of the show.

FAKE! While this headline is erroneous, the nonfiction version is even more disturbing: "Parents beat up lollipop man, 73." The 2011 telling in the *Belfast Telegraph* gets weirder the more you read it.

The "lollipop man" was a beloved Lansing, Michigan, school crossing guard, who had a penchant for handing out confections to kids. The story goes that two parents dropped off their seven-year-old boy on the corner and proceeded to urge him to attack another boy. The dutiful son punched his victim, knocking him down, and the lollipop man naturally tried to intervene. The parents flew into a rage, leaping from their car and battering the crossing guard with punches.

REAL! At first it seems that the headline for this 2012 *Miami New Times* story is phrased in an insensitive way. But as it turns out, it was the precise fact of the Guatemalan man's "sweatiness" that led to the discovery of his strange hoard.

He'd actually made it into Orlando on a flight from his native Guatemala, but was acting nervous and sweating profusely as he made his way through customs. Searching his luggage, inspectors found 172 candy-coated heroin lollipops.

WOMAN ON METH ATTACKS 75-YEAR-OLD WOMAN WITH SHOVEL

Woman on meth burns down world's oldest tree

WOMAN ON METH EXPLODES

REAL! According to the *Central Kitsap Reporter*, a Washington woman high on meth had a bit of a field day with an innocent, elderly woman in 2011.

The poor old lady arrived home to find the woman raving in her front yard, pouring gasoline over everything. The attacker swiped the house keys from the woman's hand, told her to remove her clothes so that she could set her on fire, and when she refused, picked up a shovel and thwunked her on the head.

The seventy-five-year-old woman was able to stumble into the street and wave down passersby for assistance.

REAL! New York's WPIX News told the depressing 2012 tale of the murder of "the Senator," a 3,500-year-old tree (technically the fifth oldest in the world at the time). Sarah Barnes, a twenty-six-year-old Florida woman, decided it would be fun to smoke meth with a friend while *inside* the 125-foot-tall cypress tree. She lit a fire to see, which got out of control and burned the natural treasure from the inside.

Barnes was busted because she took cell phone photos of her handiwork and shared them with friends. Reportedly she bragged, "I can't believe I burned down a tree older than Jesus."

FAKE! But it wouldn't surprise me, with all the chemicals they're putting into their bodies. The idea was inspired by the fact that newspapers are full of stories about exploding meth *labs*, which cause all kinds of havoc, like neighborhood fires, innocent lives taken, and of course, immolation deaths of the amateur, meth-making geniuses themselves.

MAN PULLS KNIFE ON FRIENDS, RUNS AWAY, HITS HEAD, INJURES SELF

Gardener stabs self with trowel, runs for help, and falls in fish pond

BREAKING NEWS

SHOPFITTER DIED AFTER FALLING FROM GIANT BUCKET OF MAYONNAISE AND STABBING HIMSELF IN THE HEART WITH ELECTRIC DRILL

REAL! The *Richmond Times-Dispatch* crafted this 2009 headline in a way that eliminated the need to actually read the article. Seriously. That's the whole story. I suppose it's worth adding that the man was drinking (naturally) and that no charges were filed.

FAKE! It could happen. You know "that friend" who has achieved such a sensational level of accident-proneness that her mishaps are worthy of their own Charlie Chaplin movie? We all have one. The kind of person whose spouse does an excellent job of child-proofing the house—even though they have no children.

REAL! It's just one of those freak accidents. Twenty-three-year-old Araz Saleh was helping a friend fix up his fast food kiosk in Oxford, England's Gloucester Green, says the 2012 article in the United Kingdom's *Daily Mail*. While affixing metal siding to the food stand, he decided to eschew a ladder in favor of standing on an industrial-sized bucket of mayonnaise.

He slipped from the bucket while the drill was running and, in the fall, managed to impale himself in the heart.

ALBEMARLE COUNTY DEPUTY ATTACKED BY ROOSTER

Smith County deputy attacked by injured cow

Mayor's deputy attacked by lions

REAL! There are a surprising number of rooster attacks on policemen in the annals of history, each similar to this 2012 story from Charlottesville, Virginia's WCAV News.

Deputy Tom Wood was attempting to serve a warrant and was actually prepared for an animal attack—a pit bull in the front yard was eyeing him warily. Wood readied his can of mace and approached the house slowly. That's when a rooster launched at him suddenly, pecking him viciously "below the belt, hard enough to double him over."

Wood squirted mace at the rooster, which appeared to have no effect.

REAL! Shreveport's KSLA News reported this 2011 story about the strange attack on an East Texas deputy by a half-ton cow.

Police found the severely injured beast on the side of a rural highway, after it had been struck by two vehicles. Deputy Robert Britton was directing traffic around the bleeding animal when it rose from the ground and charged him suddenly. Britton was knocked to the pavement, hitting his head. He eventually died of his injuries.

FAKE! The actual 1941 headline in the *New York Times* is "Mayor's deputy attacked by Lyons." See what I did there?

The real article is actually a rather boring account of an argument between Bronx president James J. Lyons and New York deputy mayor Rufus E. McGahen about city employee wage increases.

OWNER OF SEGWAY COMPANY DIES IN SEGWAY CRASH

Inventor of the chainsaw dies in chainsaw accident

CUSTOMER AT VEGAS' HEART ATTACK GRILL SUFFERS HEART ATTACK

REAL! Adding himself to a long list of ironic deaths throughout history, British businessman Jimi Heselden bought Segway, Inc., and shortly thereafter perished in a Segway accident.

Unveiled in 2001, the makers of Segways went to great lengths to convince consumers that the gyroscopically balanced, two-wheeled personal transport devices were safe.

Heselden was riding his Segway on a trail when he crashed and fell from a 30-foot cliff, according to the 2010 story in the *New York Times*.

FAKE! The first problem you encounter here is identifying a single inventor of the chainsaw. The miraculous tool as we know it was conceived in multiple steps by many people. The earliest known example of a chainsaw is a hand tool invented by two Scottish doctors in the 1700s, which used a spinning watch chain to cut up *people*. Their invention did not kill them, but it probably had a few victims nonetheless.

REAL! Irony loves company. "Heart Attack Grill" is supposed to be a playful, winking restaurant name, poking fun at the fact that eating burgers is not particularly healthy. Perhaps, however, the owners should have considered what the fallout would be if the diner lived up to its name. It doesn't help that the patron was eating a "Triple Bypass Burger" at the time of his heart attack, which, according to this 2012 story in the *Los Angeles Times*, is 1½ pounds of beef and fifteen slices of bacon in one succulent stack.

BREAKING NEWS

Delta shows porn on in-flight entertainment system during international trip

Comcast accidentally airs porn during Super Bowl

Jazz radio station airs gay porn soundtrack, apologizes

FAKE! Not true. But, Europe's Ryanair made headlines in 2012 when the head of the low-cost, Irish airline told the press that he wanted to offer an in-flight porn pay-per-view option to his patrons.

Really? Do *you* feel like going on a claustrophobic, multihour trip with the guy next to you watching porn?

Didn't think so.

REAL! It was quite the gaffe, as the 2009 *Digital Journal* article attests. Tucson-area fans, young and old, were cheering a Super Bowl XLIII touchdown by the Cardinals's Larry Fitzgerald when, moments later, they were treated to thirty seconds of full-frontal male nudity courtesy of cable porn show *Club Jenna*.

Eventually a disgruntled employee was arrested for pulling the prank, and Comcast offered a $10 credit to affected customers.

Ten bucks should make up for it.

REAL! NBC Miami told the tale of the unfortunate blunder by a U.K. radio station in 2012. The incident happened during Jazz FM's appropriately titled "Funky Sensations" program. The five-minute clip definitely had funky music going on, as well as graphic moaning, breathing, and sound effects that clearly illustrated two men getting "funky" together.

The head of programming for the station was quoted to say, "We have taken steps to ensure there will be no repeat of this incident."

LION ESCAPES, RUSHES JAIL; HIT BY BROOM, HE CRASHES CITY HALL; ENDS UP IN DOG BOX

Gorilla escapes guard, evades hot pursuit, slips away from police in Brooklyn

CIRCUS BEAR ESCAPES AND ROUTS HOBOES FROM THEIR BOX-CAR SLEEPING QUARTERS

REAL! Old-timey headlines like this 1946 headline from the *New York Times* were often awkward and long. This one is a veritable short story. Sid the lion enjoyed quite a field trip after escaping from his cage at the Sanford, Florida, zoo.

The caretaker who unlocked Sid's cage in order to sweep up made the not-so-wise decision to deliver a few whacks of his broom to the big cat, and amazingly suffered no retaliation. Sid made his way through the zoo, past the city jail, and crashed into a window of the city hall building before finally being caught in a large crate used to trap stray dogs.

FAKE! It's just a slight adaptation of another super long and very real 1916 headline from the *New York Times*: "Spy escapes guard, evades hot pursuit; Lincoln, a confessed German agent, slips away from government agent in Brooklyn."

REAL! It's the title of an extremely charming 1924 article in the *Milwaukee Journal* that reads like a children's story. Two homeless men, who self-identified as "Weary Willie and Tired Tod," were nabbed by a policeman as they made their way from a railyard. Willie claimed he smelled a bear, was afraid of them, and was getting out of there. Both the officer and Tod insisted that there were no bears in that area.

The policeman led the two men to the train car that they had been calling home, and all three were surprised to discover a small black bear sleeping underneath it. It had escaped from the circus that was in town, and it was captured again by its trainer.

The fates of Willie and Tod are unknown.

Man gets two months for pooping in store

POOPING POLITICIAN FACES PROBE

Pooping peasant popular in Spain

REAL! The 2012 United Press International headline describes a Swedish man's peculiar, week-long reign of terror in the town of Gävle, during which he smashed his landlord's window, broke into a shop to steal alcohol, and finally, caused a bit of a scene in a sporting goods store.

Apparently he marched in, pulled down his pants, did a number on the floor (number two, that is), and finished up by wiping himself with a pair of pants that were on sale.

Two months in jail and that guy should be totally normal again.

FAKE! I couldn't resist. It's similar, though, to a real 2011 headline from the *Seattle Post-Intelligencer*: "Pooping postman will keep job."

It seems a Portland mail carrier felt an emergency call of nature, dropped trou, and defecated in someone's yard like a dog. There was quite a bit of outrage, but I, for one, feel for the guy. Most people have a restroom at work. Where do these guys go, anyway?

Ultimately he kept his job, but was (wisely) assigned a different route.

REAL! The 2006 *USA Today* article gets even weirder than the headline. The "pooping peasant" is not some lovable incontinent guy from a Spanish TV show or anything rational like that. He's a pants-down, pooing figurine that is immensely popular in the Catalonia region of Spain for use in *nativity scenes*.

That's right. The baby Jesus. The Virgin Mary. Three wise guys. Some barnyard animals. And a pooper.

A German celebrity: dog defeats heat-seeking camera, George Clooney

EXPERTS: GERMAN CELEBRITY POLAR BEAR KNUT DROWNED

GERMAN CELEBRITY BUNNY MEETS UNTIMELY DEMISE WHEN STEPPED ON BY TV CAMERAMAN

FAKE! It's awfully ridiculous-sounding, I know, but the real version is just as weird: "A German celebrity: cow defeats heat-seeking camera, George Clooney of bulls" was the headline of a bizarre-yet-riveting 2011 story in Abu Dhabi's *The National*. On her way to a slaughterhouse, Yvonne the cow decided to smash her way through a 8,000-volt electric fence and disappear into the woods.

She evaded capture for three months, despite a 10,000-euro reward for her apprehension, a shoot-to-kill order to hunters, multiple helicopter searches with a high-end heat-sensing camera, and, best of all, the depositing into the woods of an irresistible bull ox ("the George Clooney of bulls"). Yvonne is now living out her days in an animal sanctuary.

REAL! The 2011 ABC News story tells of a fluffy, lovable-looking bear cub that captivated a nation when he was rejected by his mother. "Knut" was a popular figure, appearing on magazine covers, in his own movie, and plastered all over merchandise.

Illness caused Knut's brain to swell. He fainted into the pond in his enclosure and drowned.

REAL! "Til" was the name of a baby rabbit that had Germany mesmerized due in large part to his cuteness, but in larger part to the fact that he was born without bunny ears.

As the 2012 *Winnipeg Free Press* article puts it, Til was "a rising star on Germany's celebrity animal scene." A media orgy had begun, and would ultimately cut Til's red carpet career short.

The bunny was nestled underneath a pile of hay, out of sight, when a cameraman stepped backward, crushing and killing him instantly.

What a *heel*.

BREAKING NEWS

Scientist develops 'anti-stupidity' pill

Danes developing pill to cure ugliness

Common pill could cure racism

REAL! German scientist Hans Hilger-Ropers splashed onto the scene in 2006, being featured in stories like this one from *Sky News*, because he claimed to be making progress on a pill that would prevent cretinism, oafdom, foolery, boobishness, and buffoonery the world over. He had tested it on fruit flies and found increased intelligence.

I have two questions.

One, how do you get fruit flies to take a pill? And two, whatever happened to Hilger-Ropers and this promised percipience pill? Personally, I think he developed it, took it himself, built a time machine or spaceship or something, and is long gone.

FAKE! That is extremely far-fetched. Scientists in Denmark *are* attempting to develop a pill that counters a societal ugliness, though. They may be on to something with their new drug Nalmafene, which many believe will be the world's first pill to cure alcoholism.

The jury is still out, but in tests, Nalmafene-taking alcoholics consume 50 percent less booze than their counterparts.

REAL! According to the *Hamilton Spectator*, an Oxford University lab test of a pill for heart disease demonstrated that it reduced implicit racial prejudice in subjects.

It's a long way from being a "racism cure," but the findings have interesting connotations. The drug is thought to reduce prejudice-based fear in the brain's amygdala, and subconscious fear is thought by many to be one of the foundations of racism.

MICHAEL JACKSON'S HAIR EXPLODES

Michael Jackson's hair to be turned into diamonds

Michael Jackson's hair clump to become roulette ball

FAKE! It would be a little of a stretch to say that happened. However, as many of you will recall, hundreds of newspapers ran this headline in 1984: "Michael Jackson's hair catches fire."

The notorious incident occurred while the King of Pop was filming a Pepsi commercial. While performing "Billie Jean," he danced too close to a pyrotechnics display. His hair and jacket caught fire, and he was rushed to a hospital. It's widely speculated that the third-degree burns and subsequent treatment contributed largely to the singer's addiction to painkillers.

REAL! Our wide world is full of wonders that we seldom expect, don't you think? Illinois company LifeGem sells man-made diamonds molecularly identical to naturally found ones. As if that's not cool enough, the company makes the diamonds out of *hair samples from real people*.

This 2009 article in the *Telegraph* reported that LifeGem had acquired a lock of Michael Jackson's hair and would be making diamonds from it. Time to go check eBay!

REAL! Proving that there is no established limit for weirdness, an online gambling company shelled out nearly $11,000 for a wad of Michael Jackson's hair in 2011 and announced plans to forge it into a roulette ball, according to this Reuters article.

The hair, fished out of a hotel shower drain by a Jackson fan in the '80s, will be encased in a ball of "the highest professional standards," says the gambling website. "We want Michael to rock and 'ROLL' forever."

Yikes.

COPS: MAN TRIED TO 'FIX' PRICELESS PAINTING WITH BUTTER KNIFE

Cops: Colorado woman punches, rubs her buttocks against $30 million painting

COPS SAY ARTWORK GOT UNDER MAN'S SKIN, SHOE

FAKE! The man was even loonier than that. The real 2011 MSNBC headline goes a little something like this: "Cops: man tries to fix hernia with butter knife."

That's right. A sixty-three-year-old Glendale man was tired of waiting for his hernia surgery, so he went out back, sat in a lawn chair, and proceeded to try and take care of it himself. Police were bewildered to find him sitting calmly with a 6-inch butter knife protruding from his abdomen.

REAL! Everyone's a critic. Thirty-six-year-old Carmen Tisch was certainly expressing herself when, according to this 2012 MSNBC article, she punched and scratched a $30 million Clyfford Still painting at a museum in Denver. Not content to stop there, she pulled down her pants and rubbed her naked derriere all over the artwork. Still not satisfied, she proceeded to try and urinate on the piece, but was so drunk that she missed entirely.

REAL! The *Chicago Tribune* editor was feeling saucy when he penned this 2007 headline.

The article describes a strange scene in which twenty-one-year-old Timothy Kubena was offended by Ottavio Vannini's seventeenth-century painting "The Triumph of David," which depicts a biblical scene of the triumphant David holding Goliath's head. Kubena proceeded to kick the Milwaukee Art Museum's $300,000 painting repeatedly in the bottom-right corner. A museum staff member grabbed Kubena by the sweater in an effort to stop him, but Kubena simply shrugged out of the garment and continued his assault.

When he was done, Kubena reportedly said, "I come in peace," took off his shoes, and lay down on the floor until police arrived.

476 PEOPLE STABBED WITH SYRINGES IN CHINA

L.A. man who shushes moviegoer is stabbed with meat thermometer

BREAKING NEWS

KINDERGARTENER STABBED BY CLASSMATE WITH SHARPENED CRAYON

REAL! The *Arizona Republic* ran this 2009 headline about an extremely chilling spate of needle attacks in China.

Labeled as an example of "ethnic cleansing," the stabbings targeted Han Chinese almost exclusively. No sudden diseases or infections seemed to pop up in the victims, and it's largely believed that the syringes contained no toxins but were simply used to incite fear and terror.

REAL! A Los Angeles man was trying to enjoy a screening of *Shutter Island* in 2010 when the woman in front of him began using her mobile phone. So, according to the New York *Daily News*, he asked her to turn it off.

Big mistake. The woman's boyfriend got up, walked out of the theater, went to his car, retrieved a recently purchased meat thermometer, returned to the darkened room, and stabbed the complainer in the neck. Another moviegoer attempted to intervene and was also stabbed with the thermometer for his trouble.

Both victims made full recoveries, and the suspect was arrested.

FAKE! Okay, I admit it. I did it. It never made the news, but I'm guilty of the crime. It didn't break the skin, though. She just cried. And my Burnt Umber was broken.

BREAKING NEWS

Bear bites Florida woman in the butt

JILTED LOVER BITES WOMAN ON THE BUTT

Lawyer bites woman's butt in court, is arrested

REAL! WTSP Tampa tells the 2012 story of a very eventful session of dog-walking had by a fifty-seven-year-old Longwood, Florida, woman. As she passed some trash bins, she noticed a 300-plus–pound bear and her cub. She tried to continue on nonchalantly, but her dog, as dogs do, confronted the bear.

The woman fled, tripped, and fell. The huge beast sank its jaws into her behind and, thankfully, moved on. She has since recovered.

REAL! When a thirty-nine-year-old personal assistant tried to break up with her boyfriend in the coastal town of Kota Kinabalu, he did not take it well, according to the 2006 story in the *Malaysia Star*. He punched her in the nose and, as she struggled to get away, bit her on the buttocks. Thinking quickly, she told him that she changed her mind. He calmed down and eventually left. She went straight to the police.

FAKE! It could have happened if the guy wasn't caught early on. In 1990, North Carolina's *Dispatch* told the story of an aspiring law student, Chep Hurth, who decided that biting women's rear ends in bars was an effective way to break the ice. One fine evening, at a bar, he did just that to fellow law student Maya Brodie.

Brodie sued Hurth for damages, including humiliation, pain, and three days of missed class. Hurth was flabbergasted and testified in court that he had bitten strange women on the butt in bars before, and that they hadn't minded.

Father, son murdered 30 years apart

PLANE CRASHES KILL FATHER, SON ON SAME DAY—40 YEARS APART

Lightning kills father, son 48 years apart

REAL! Washington's *Tri City Herald* ran the 1977 story about history repeating itself in the most gruesome of ways.

In 1947, when Harry Zavakos was a young man, his father was gunned down in front of their house and killed instantly. In 1952, Zavakos received a telephone call that informed him he would die in the same manner as his father. The killer was caught, and Zavakos moved on with his life.

Thirty years later, in 1977, Harry was returning home after his shift at a bowling alley when he was gunned down. He was shot at the same time of night, and *in the exact same location* as his father, and was killed instantly.

FAKE! Didn't happen. In 2007/2008, however, a Canadian father and son each died in a plane crash, five months apart.

REAL! The 2011 NBC News story is especially eerie. When Stephen Rooney was five years old, his father went fishing in Fortescue, New Jersey, where he was struck by lightning and killed instantly.

Forty-eight years later, Rooney was having a barbecue with his family in Hammonton, New Jersey. He stepped away from the group to smoke a cigar, was struck by lightning, and was killed instantly.

The creepiest part? Family members reported that the last thing he said to them was:

"Don't worry. Lightning never strikes twice."

Canada is part of the
United States

IS NORTH
DAKOTA
REALLY
A STATE?

GIVE US BACK TO THE
INDIANS, OHIO NEVER
REALLY A STATE

FAKE! Don't be ridiculous. Of course it's not. In fact, the *Sun* ran this helpful headline in 1957: "Canada is not part of the United States."

REAL! It at first seems like a really inane question for a news article to ask, but upon inspection, MSNBC's 2011 inquiry turns out to be completely legitimate.

An elderly Grand Forks resident noticed that North Dakota's constitution does not meet requirements as set forth by the federal constitution, which, he argues, makes the upper Dakota's statehood illegitimate.

Lawmakers have begun the process of amending the constitution to keep the state within governmental guidelines.

REAL! The snarky 1953 *Youngstown Vindicator* headline was thoroughly accurate.

In January of that year, officials realized that the U.S. Congress had never formally issued a resolution admitting Ohio to the Union, meaning that it was never officially a state.

In August of 1953, President Eisenhower signed a resolution declaring Ohio to be a state in the Union and declared that it would take place retroactively: in March of 1803.

BREAKING NEWS

Seattle woman marries warehouse

Woman proves love for Eiffel Tower with commitment ceremony

Nevada woman 'marries' specific 3.7-mile stretch of highway

REAL! Unlike most "object fetishists," you could say that Babylonia Aivaz, the subject of this 2012 *Wisconsin Gazette* story, was not truly in love with her betrothed at all and only got "married" for ulterior motives.

Aivaz was an Occupy Seattle protester and organized the wedding to protest a 100-plus-year-old building's impending demolition to make way for an expensive high-rise. She claimed that corporations had been given the same rights as people, and therefore buildings should have rights too.

REAL! The 2009 ABC News story revolves around Erika Eiffel, a San Francisco native who is one of the growing number of "objectum sexuals" in the world—people who are attracted to objects rather than other people.

Erika, who took the last name "Eiffel" after marrying the Paris landmark, had previously been in love with a bridge and an F-15.

FAKE! That particular story hasn't happened yet, but the ranks of objectum sexuals seem to be growing every day.

There are multiple public reports of "open" o-sexuals and their relationships with inanimate objects, including but not limited to: a roller coaster, a fence, a pillow, a laundry basket, a pick-up truck, and the Berlin Wall.

It's gotten me thinking. I really do love my cowboy hat . . .

SWALLOWS, DIES . . .

Just a little bit of research proves that animals will try to swallow anything, and humans are the worst of the lot. Sometimes swallowing a tiny object will kill you, and sometimes a person can swallow a ridiculous amount of nonfood items and survive.

First, some of the casualties . . .

MAN SWALLOWS DENTURES DURING SEX AND DIES

Malaysia's *Star Online*, February 2, 2012

That's one heck of a way to go. A seventy-four-year-old Taiwanese man got a little too excited while engaging the services of a sixty-two-year-old prostitute, and swallowed his own teeth.

MAN SWALLOWS BEE, DIES OF SUFFOCATION

Oklahoma's *Altus Times*, August 14, 1983

In a case of awful luck, a sixty-year-old Michigan man inadvertently swallowed a bee after it flew into his beer can. The bee stung him in the throat from the inside, which caused it to swell and cut off his air completely.

BABY SWALLOWS PEBBLE, DIES; CHILD SWALLOWS DETERGENT, DIES; GIRL SWALLOWS WASP, DIES; MAN SWALLOWS BAG OF DRUGS, DIES; SWALLOWS CROCHETING HOOK, WOMAN DIES; MAN SWALLOWS HEROIN-FILLED CONDOMS, DIES

Chicago Tribune, October 11, 1936; *Toledo Blade*, August 27, 1971; *Hartford Courant*, September 12, 1934; *The Vancouver Province*, August 3, 2008; *Lewiston Daily Sun*, May 24, 1932; North Carolina's *The Robesonian*, September 25, 1997

There are hundreds more, involving people perishing from swallowing toothpicks, magnets, toys, poison, tobacco, bleach, balloons, keys, marbles, peanuts, chloroform, glass, knives, lye, acid, and pesticide.

HERBERT THE WALRUS SWALLOWS BALL, DIES

Sarasota Journal, March 17, 1953

Unfortunately, Herbert's not the only one. Nyla the hippo, Algae the porpoise, and several other animals have died swallowing rubber balls, indicating that a real zoo-pidemic is going on . . .

LOSES THE GOLF MATCH WHEN SNAKE SWALLOWS BALL

Pittsburgh Press, August 15, 1913

In a very strange case of a sort of real-life Aesop's fable, a man lost a closely contested golf game when a snake swallowed his ball on the green. The snake was ruled a legitimate hazard, and he lost a stroke. The article notes: "The snake was run down and killed and the ball will be placed on exhibition."

MAN EATS COCAINE FROM BROTHER'S BUTT, DIES

Honolulu's KITV News, December 21, 2011

Ah, the *pièce de résistance*. I'm telling you, newspaper editors could easily transition into comedy writing. When two South Carolina brothers were pulled over for suspected drug possession, they were put in the back of a squad car. One had been hiding an ounce of cocaine in his rear end and convinced the other to swallow it. The loving brother complied, and died from it.

To be continued . . .

PENIS-BITING FISH GO WILD AS MEN PEE IN RIVER

Fish that 'looks like a penis' banned from textbooks

Fish swims into boy's penis

REAL! The headline has a bit of a comic feel to it, but the real story, as reported in 2001 by South Africa's *Independent Online*, is deadly serious.

Two Papua, New Guinea, men were urinating in a river when deadly "piranha-like" fish attacked them, tearing viciously at their private parts. Both men bled to death.

It's believed that the penis-biters had migrated from Indonesia, sensing prey by chemical changes in the water. The men's urine triggered their attack instinct, and they pounced.

FAKE! Look out, Martha! Here comes a school of penis-looking fish!

But seriously, it's not far-fetched. Schools have forbidden far more innocuous things than pictures of fish. Recently, some American schools have kept the students' best interests at heart and banned cake, Halloween, hugging, Ugg boots, birthdays, and my personal favorite: being best friends. You know, to protect the feelings of the left-out.

REAL! Though this story is documented, reported, and much written about (such as in this 2008 article in the *Sun*), I *still* don't know if I believe it.

According to a young boy's account, he was cleaning his fish tank at his home in India. He felt an urgent call of nature and proceeded to go and relieve himself while holding a small fish in his hand. The fish wriggled from his grasp, and *into his penis*. The little animal, about ¾-inch long, proceeded to work its way up the boy's urethra and eventually wound up in his bladder.

He went to the hospital, where doctors located the fish. They first attempted to remove it *through the penis* with forceps, and when that didn't work, they employed a special tool used for removing kidney stones, with success.

SCIENTIST MAKES POOP BURGER

Washington scientist opens up a can of constipated worms

'GLOWING' DOG POOP CONFUSES MIT SCIENTISTS

REAL! You may not want it to be real, but it is. As this 2011 *Huffington Post* article attests, Japanese scientist Mitsuyuki Ikeda managed to create a synthetic burger, the bulk of which is pure protein extracted from human feces.

Combine the protein with some soya and steak sauce for taste, and you've got one bona fide shitwich.

But is it vegetarian?

REAL! It's easy to see why the 1994 *Kitchener-Waterloo Record* headline was phrased so humorously. It was the title of a Dave Barry column in which he exhaustively described the time he spent with a scientist who exclusively studied worm poop.

FAKE! You should know that MIT scientists are *never* confused about anything. Buncha know-it-alls. Take Matthew Mazzota for example, who was the inspiration for this bogus headline. In his MIT lab, he figured out how to make a converter that turns dog poop into energy for public lamps. He installed one in a Cambridge dog park, and the droppings deposited in the contraption by canine owners consistently powered the lantern.

I guess you could say he saw dog poop in a new light.

TEEN TEXTING WHILE WALKING FALLS INTO OPEN MANHOLE

Texting while walking claims another victim, woman falls off pier

BREAKING NEWS

ARIZONA MAN WAS TEXTING WHEN HE WALKED OFF CLIFF

REAL! I imagine people across the street were quite shocked when they saw fifteen-year-old Staten Island teen Alex Longueria, who was walking with a friend and texting on her cell phone, completely disappear from view. Just like something out of a cartoon, Longueria stepped directly into an open manhole, says the 2009 KTLA News story.

She escaped the incident with relatively minor cuts, scrapes, and bruises. If I were her father, I'd say she learned a valuable lesson and will likely watch where she's going from now on. Longueria's parents, however, cried foul and launched a lawsuit against the city. (The workers had just opened the manhole and were a few feet away fetching cones from the truck when the girl fell in.)

REAL! Walking right off the end of a pier is perhaps as comically iconic as falling into a manhole. According to this 2012 Yahoo! News article, South Bend, Indiana's Bonnie Miller did just that. Rather than retreating into a cave of embarrassment like some of the texting-while-walking accident-prones are doing (like the woman who walked right into a shopping mall fountain), Miller has bravely taken to the public eye to warn people of the perilousness of palpating a personal device while perambulating.

FAKE! But it could happen to you! Beware! Is sending that winky-face emoticon really worth your *life*? And while you're at it, avoid texting while cooking, working out, or delivering a baby.

BREAKING NEWS

Stab victim 'continued masturbating'

BEVERLY HILLS POLICE CHIEF CALLS STAB VICTIM A GIGOLO

Critical condition for Mickey Mouse stabbed by 14-year-old boy at Disney resort

REAL! To read this 2007 story in the *Brisbane Times*, some sort of otherworldly urge came over an Australian man, powerful enough to send him on a self-pleasuring spree that continued even after he was stabbed twice. Perhaps it was the large amount of amphetamines that he had taken.

He was in a friend's apartment when the "masturbation marathon" began, and she immediately objected, due to the fact that she had two small children at home. When he wouldn't stop, she stabbed him with a kitchen knife twice in the shoulder. The man merely fled into her garage and continued his half-naked and bloody business until police found him.

REAL! Just looking at the headline, you'd think the chief was some kind of jerk, insulting a poor victim like that. But, upon deeper inspection of the 1958 article from South Carolina's *News and Courier*, you realize that the "victim" was a gangster-style con artist who regularly beat up movie star Lana Turner.

It was Turner's fourteen-year-old daughter who stabbed the man, most would say, with excellent reason. The guy was violent and was known to court wealthy women, squeeze money from them, and move on.

You could say that the Beverly Hills police chief was pretty much on the money.

FAKE! While that headline is fallacious, you might have read this 1986 one from the *Milwaukee Sentinel*: "Jeepers! Mickey is stab victim." In that story, "Mickey" was indeed stabbed by a fourteen-year-old boy, and was even reported to be in "critical condition," but the victim was not living. It was a 40-foot-tall balloon.

Health officials: pools, diarrhea not good mix

1 in 5 Americans pee in the pool

Two hundred gallons of rancid toilet water dumped in starlet's swimming pool

REAL! You'd think such a notion would fit firmly in the realm of "too obvious to report," but in 2001, the Omaha *World-Herald* didn't agree.

The summer before, Omaha dealt with an outbreak of a nasty parasitic disease called cryptosporidiosis, thanks to several infected swimming pools. And by infected, I mean they had diarrhea in them. Chlorine is tough, but not *that* tough.

All in all, it was a crappy situation.

REAL! The 2009 Fox News story is quick to point out that the 20 percent of us who apparently count pool-urination as a hobby are *just the ones who admit it*. Who knows what the real figure is? Gross!

Health experts have pointed out that chemicals in the pool are *not* effective at preventing potential negative effects. In fact, urine (and sweat) can, in some cases, combine with disinfectants to create a harmful cocktail that can lead to undesirable things such as asthma and bladder cancer.

Swimming, anyone?

FAKE! While that would be a terrible prank, in 1949 similar headlines abounded, such as this one from the *Los Angeles Times*: "Fragrant toilet water to be dumped into swimming pool for Rita and Aly."

Movie star Rita Hayworth's impending wedding to the exotic Prince Aly Khan had captivated the nation. The extravagant affair had all kinds of ridiculous touches, not the least of which was 200 gallons of "toilet water" being dumped into the swimming pool.

It's important to note, here, that "toilet water" at the time meant "eau de toilette," or perfumed water, not water from toilets.

Missionary position puts Haverty on top

DOGGY STYLE IS NOTHING TO SNIFF AT

MEXICAN BOMB A BLACK HAND JOB

REAL! Proof that 1961 was a much more innocent time, this article in the *Hartford Courant* is about canine fashion. It's a penetrating profile of certain well-heeled, fancy, Fifth Avenue dogs and their ostentatious owners.

It's incredible to think that more than fifty years ago, delicate booties, silken pajamas, and mink coats were already trending as doggy-wear.

REAL! It took me three minutes of my brain heating up, and filtering through several disturbing images, before I began to understand what this headline was really referring to. For example, it's *not* trying to tell you that "Mexican Bomb" is the newest slang for black hand jobs.

The 1909 article in the *Detroit Free Press* was trying to tell us that a bombing in Monterey, Mexico, was the work of a super-secret, ultra-dangerous militant gang called the Black Hand Society.

I wonder how many Black Hand jobs there were before the action climaxed.

BREAKING NEWS

Burger King worker arrested for robbing own Burger King

McDonald's worker arrested for serving cop salty hamburger

Taco Bell worker arrested for handcuffing himself to woman he wanted to date

FAKE! "BK" must be doing something right. Based on crime data in the newspapers, Burger King employees aren't getting in trouble with anywhere near the frequency of other fast food chains (like Taco Bell and McDonald's).

In fact, a CBS story made the rounds in 2012 about how Burger King employees in Fort Lauderdale, Florida, *foiled* an attempted robbery of their location, "body-slamming" the perpetrator and holding him until police arrived.

REAL! That's a new offense to put on the books. Georgia McDonald's worker Kendra Bull allegedly served a hamburger to a policeman that she had purposely overloaded with salt and pepper. According to the cop, it was salty enough to send him to the hospital. Bull was arrested.

She argued that she accidentally knocked salt into a bowl of hamburger meat she was preparing, and that she ate one of the salty patties herself and felt just fine.

REAL! Dalton, Georgia, Taco Bell employee Jason Dean pulled into the parking lot as an eighteen-year-old coworker left her shift and quickly slapped one handcuff on her wrist, and the other on his own. She screamed for help, and the police were called. He was charged with false imprisonment. According to the 2011 story in the Chatanooga *Times Free Press*, he had tried on numerous occasions to get her to agree to go on a date with him, always unsuccessfully.

You gotta give him credit for thinking "outside the bun."

MAN GETS THIRTY-YEAR SENTENCE FOR TOSSING A BEER BOTTLE

Virginia woman faces 50 years behind bars for decapitating piglet

Cop killer gets 10,000 years in jail

FAKE! The real sentence you can get for tossing beer bottles is much, much better. In 2006, Municipal Court Judge David Hostetler of Coshocton, Ohio, convicted two men of throwing beer bottles and denting a car. He gave them a choice: sixty days in jail . . . or an hour-long walk up and down Main Street dressed head-to-toe in women's clothes.

The men opted for the drag walk and served their sentence in dresses, wigs, and full makeup. They didn't make it a full hour—an onlooker threw a bottle at them, hitting one. The assailant was arrested, and the two men set free.

I wonder what sentence the judge gave the new guy.

REAL! The 2011 CBS News headline is real, but a little bit misleading. Yes, Ashley Fowler decided to behead her ex-boyfriend's piglet and leave its head on his porch as a sort of sick "screw you." But fifty years is the *maximum* possible sentence she could have been assigned. Nobody ever thought it would actually be that long.

She wound up getting ninety days for the crime.

REAL! In 1973, Eugene Spencer Jr. was indeed handed a 10,000-year prison term for the murder of a police officer, as the *Chicago Tribune* headline attests. It's happened at least one more time since then: in 1981, Dudley Wayne Kyzer, convicted of killing his wife, his mother-in-law, and a university student, received 10,000 years *plus two life sentences* for the crimes.

BREAKING NEWS

British woman weds dolphin

TWO MINOR GIRLS MARRIED OFF TO FROGS

Tennessee man marries goat

REAL! The *Sydney Morning Herald* spun this storybook tale of interspecies love in a 2005 issue. A British woman, Sharon Tendler, had been traveling to Israel two times a year for fifteen years, just to swim with the "love of her life," a trained male dolphin named Cindy. Finally, she decided to take the "plunge" into the dolphin pool and marry Cindy.

She was quoted to say, "I made a dream come true. And I am not a pervert."

REAL! The strange scenario was reported by the *Times of India* in 2009, and described the ritual marriage of two little girls to frogs in the village of Puducherry. Local residents told the press that the marriages were in order to ward off evil spirits and prevent disease in the village.

How marrying a frog is a way to *avoid* disease, I can't figure out.

FAKE! I am confident that the fine folks in Tennessee would never conduct themselves in such a way. The fib was inspired by a real headline from BBC News: "Sudan man forced to 'marry' goat."

Apparently, a man woke up to strange noises and found a stranger . . . um, *with* his goat. He apprehended the pawky paramour and delivered him to the village elders, who decided the suspect should be forced to pay a dowry and marry the goat.

Poor goat.

JUST THE COLD, HARD, FARTS

For a company whose motto has been "Don't be evil," Google has certainly been avidly pursuing a diabolical plan to index and make searchable "all of the world's information." Google News has been busy scanning and converting tens of thousands of old newspapers into online text. Because automated programs are used and the quality of old newspaper print can be low, headlines are often mistranslated with hilarious results. Here, find actual Google headline results that prove Google's scanners have a sense of humor.

RELEASE THE FARTS

Portsmouth Times, January 3, 1958

*facts

GERMANS SHOULD FACE FARTS

Milwaukee Journal, April 19, 1962

*facts

KEATING KEEPS PINPOINTING PAINFUL FARTS

Miami News, February 4, 1963

*facts

FORD URGED TO MAKE FARTS PUBLIC

Pittsburgh Post-Gazette, October 4, 1974

*facts

THE FARTS BEHIND FILTER-TIP CIGARETTES

Palm Beach Post, June 25, 1957

*facts

WITHHOLDING OF FARTS DEPLORED

Spokesman-Review, January 20, 1966

*facts

REV. HAND ADMITS REPORT BASED ON SECOND-HAND FARTS

Sunday Morning Star, September 30, 1934

*facts

ENERGY PROGRAM'S FARTS ARE 'BRUTAL'

St. Joseph Gazette, March 18, 1977

*facts

CHURCHILL FARTS WITH HALF-CIGAR

Edmonton Journal, February 1, 1941

*parts

RESTRICTIONS ON ATOMIC FARTS ADDED TO BILL

Portsmouth Times, May 7, 1954

*parts

Plus, two that Google's scanner *really* fouled up . . .

BURYING THE .AN TWO FARTS A DAD DIRT AT FARTED

Boca Raton News, March 23, 1972

*"Burying the bus—An unidentified youth hurls a clod of dirt at an old school bus . . . "

. . . GUNSHOT DEATH .DRAT JUMBLED FACTS BAFFLE .FARTS .RAFFLE

News-Dispatch, January 23, 1952

*"Authorities investigate gunshot death: jumbled facts baffle police after woman dies from wound"

And finally, the best of the lot . . .

'TRUST IN GOD, STALE FARTS,' IKE ADVISES

Schenectady Gazette, July 4, 1959

*state facts

BREAKING NEWS

Allies beat off

MILF BRACES FOR FAP OFFENSIVE

Wet GOP whacks off

REAL! One fine morning in 1944, breakfasters were treated to those three little words at the top of page six of the St. Petersburg *Evening Independent*, an unfortunate shortening of "Allies beat off Nazis at beachhead."

I suppose either way you read it, it's happy news.

REAL! If there's anybody out there who is puzzled as to why there's anything funny about "MILF" or "FAP," I applaud you. Enjoy your sweet innocence and have fun playing shuffleboard with the other grannies this afternoon.

Certainly the editor of this 2011 article in the *Manila Mail* isn't "down" with the parlance of the Internet generation, or she would have phrased things differently. "MILF" here refers to the Moro Islamic Liberation Front, a militant group in the Southern Philippines. "FAP" in this case is a bastardization of "AFP," or Armed Forces of the Philippines.

FAKE! That is a late-night, pay-per-view movie for which I *would not* opt in. Folks did read this similar lead line in an old issue of the *Chicago Tribune*: "Whet GOP ax to whack off whoopee funds." For the life of me, I can't figure out what that means, but I'm sure it was important news on January 4, 1953.

Pope bars perfume

POPE COMMISSIONS CUSTOM-BLENDED EAU DE COLOGNE

Scented pope is altering Vatican atmosphere

REAL! Pope Pius XI had a particular sensitivity to stink, according to this 1923 article in the *Reading Eagle*. Apparently, two over-scented "Parisiennes" left him with a headache for two days. He gave strict orders to the Bishop of Paris that he would "refuse to admit in his presence heavily perfumed women."

REAL! What a difference ninety years make! Pope Benedict does not object to smells, it seems, in the same way that Pius XI did. In fact, he loves them—and loves them enough to commission his own bespoke cologne from celebrity scentsmith Sylvia Casoli.

The papal aroma is one of verbena, lime tree, and grass, says Casoli in the 2012 *Guardian* story, to celebrate the high-hatted one's love of nature.

FAKE! Although the sentiment is no doubt true, since the current pope has been strolling the corridors with his new cologne on . . .

The real headline from further back, a 1978 issue of North Carolina's *Star-News*, is equally odd: "Skiing pope is altering Vatican atmosphere." It's a funny story about how John Paul II, the first non-Italian pope in over 400 years, was turning out to be a little more outside-the-box than the Vatican staff had expected. The newly appointed Polish pope was more gregarious than his predecessors, had a penchant for exercise (including skiing and canoeing), preferred bacon and eggs in the morning to the typical coffee and roll, and had a predilection for beer over wine.

Tony the Tiger in trouble with the law over flakes

LAWYERS ARGUE FOR ACCUSED KILLER CUCKOO FOR COCOA PUFFS

"LUCKY CHARMS KILLER" SPRINKLES VICTIMS' BODIES WITH MARSHMALLOWS

REAL! Of course it's preposterous that a cartoon character could be charged in court. The Kellogg company was taken to trial though, and Tony the Tiger was named in the suit, making this 1990 headline from the *Orlando Sentinel* essentially true.

Attorneys general from six states claimed that promises made by the smiling tiger in commercials about the healthiness of Frosted Flakes were fundamentally untrue. Kellogg never admitted wrongdoing, and Tony the Tiger made no apology, but the company did settle, paying $30,000 each to Texas, Iowa, California, Minnesota, Wisconsin, and Florida.

REAL! The 2012 Fox News story is as silly as it sounds. A special hearing was convened in which a judge heard from a small army of lawyers arguing for and against an incarcerated, accused killer's right to eat Cocoa Puffs cereal.

Alleged multimurderer Holly Grigsby was in custody awaiting trial and was forced to live on a "bland" jailhouse diet. She demanded sugary cereal and was denied. This, her lawyers argue, was a violation of her rights.

Sugary junk food has been used to make "prison alcohol," a hobby for which Grigsby herself had already been busted.

FAKE! It's completely invented; just a product of my disturbed imagination. General Mills, if you'd like to take this idea and use it as an outside-the-box advertising campaign, it's all yours!

FETUSES FOUND IN LUGGAGE AT MIAMI AIRPORT

3 fetuses found hanging in field

BREAKING NEWS

300 FETUSES FOUND AT BANGKOK TEMPLE

REAL! The *Boston Herald* ran this extremely disturbing 2012 report on a pair of women and their truly bizarre baggage.

The two unborn babies were sealed in jars in the women's bags, where they were discovered by customs agents on their return from Cuba. The ladies, both elderly, explained that they were given the jars by a "babalao," or Santeria priest, and instructed to hand them off to contacts in the States.

Officials believe the fetuses were for use in some sort of dark ritual.

REAL! That's right. Three fetuses *hanging*—as in by a noose—in a California field. Turns out, the 1982 *Boston Globe* story explains, they were placed there by anti-abortion activists in a very successful attempt to create a disturbing visual.

Why they chose a remote meadow for the display is a mystery, however, and made for a pretty shocking discovery by an unsuspecting hunter.

FAKE! That's ridiculous. Three hundred fetuses in the back of a Buddhist temple in Thailand? The number is much higher than that. The *Daily News* reported in 2010: "More than 2,000 human fetuses found in Buddhist temple in Thailand," and MSNBC put it like this: "2,000 fetuses discovered at Bangkok temple."

A woman was found guilty of performing illegal abortions, and stockpiling the evidence.

Meth found in a child's happy meal

54 BAGS OF METH FOUND INSIDE WOMAN'S GENITALS

Methamphetamine found inside cans of cheese sauce, jalapeños

REAL! NBC's Channel 14 News in Evansville, Indiana, ran the headline in 2011, but went on to say that the "happy meal" was on the floor of a car that was pulled over, not served by drug-dealing McDonald's employees.

Kinda misleading, if you ask me!

FAKE! But, according to an AOL News story, police did find fifty-four bags of *heroin* in a woman's genitals in 2011. Oh, and they also found thirty-one empty bags, eight prescription pills, and fifty-one dollars and twenty-two cents in her vagina.

REAL! According to this story from the *Los Angeles Times*, a Mexican citizen claimed to have gone grocery shopping in Mexico when he was stopped at a border crossing. Police thought his canned goods were a little heavy and submitted them to an X-ray.

Two cans of cheese sauce and one of jalapeños turned out to contain $140,000 worth of methamphetamine. That would have made some *expensive* (and deadly) nachos!

DOG MEAT PUT ON MENU FOR NAZIS

Phoenix restaurant serves dog burgers despite protests

Puppy meat no different than pork, celebrity chef argues

REAL! At first glance, the headline seems to me to be suggesting that some Nazis went into a restaurant where they weren't welcome and were sneakily served dog meat. However, the context is entirely different.

The *St. Petersburg Times* article is from 1940, when World War II had just begun and the United States was not involved yet. Dog meat was legalized in Germany in anticipation of food shortages during what everyone could already tell would be a protracted war.

Even long after the war, many Germans held on to their taste for canines.

FAKE! The fake headline was inspired by a real *San Diego Union-Tribune* headline from 2010 about a Phoenix eatery: "Restaurant serves lion burgers despite protests." That's right, lion.

Turns out serving lion is perfectly legal, as long as it's not from an endangered population, meaning African lions are okay, but Asiatic ones are not. The restaurateur in question only served forty lion burgers for a special occasion, but he was still treated with a group of protesters out front, and even a couple of death threats.

REAL! The 2011 story from Toronto's *Globe and Mail* is for serious. British celebrity chef Hugh Fearnley-Whittingstall *did* in fact publicly argue that puppy meat is comparable to pork. However, he was not arguing from a taste standpoint; he was trying to make an ethical point.

Fearnley-Whittingstall, like a growing number of ethicists, argues that where we draw the line when it comes to "acceptable" meats to eat is rather arbitrary and not based on legitimate reasoning. Pigs have long been established to be as intelligent as dogs, and pundits in the meat debate say that our rejection of dog meat and approval of pork is, at its core, hypocrisy.

MAN FAILS SOBRIETY TEST, BLAMES HAIR LOSS TREATMENT

Man says he failed sobriety test because he was kissing on 'a drunk chick'

FLORIDA WOMAN BLAMES HER 'BIG BREASTS' FOR FAILING SOBRIETY TEST

FAKE! It would definitely be hard to pull that excuse off. It seems to work for failing other tests, though: Brazilian soccer player Romário failed a doping test in 2007 and blamed it on the fact that he was taking Propecia to stave off baldness.

Hair-loss treatments like Propecia have proven to be effective screeners for people looking to conceal steroid use.

REAL! According to the 2012 *Lebanon Daily Record* article, the nineteen-year-old kid seemed to think his excuse for failing the breathalyzer was pretty airtight.

Officers maintained that he was visibly drunk himself, however, and failed multiple sobriety tests, not the least of which was to come up with a "sober" excuse for his intoxicated appearance and erratic driving.

REAL! When Maureen Jane Raymond was stopped for suspected drunk driving and asked to perform some tasks to test her sobriety, she made the completely valid point that having very big boobs can interfere with her balance, according to this 2012 Fox News story.

That was about the extent of her ability to blame her drunkenness on her bosom, however. When the officer asked her to walk a straight line, she began to dance instead. As the policeman continued to encourage her to perform the tests, she continued to comment on her breasts and attempted to take off her shirt and show them to him.

She was arrested and charged with DUI.

TINY PENIS WINS BIG COMPETITION

School surprised by 20ft penis

BREAKING NEWS

GIANT PENIS MYSTERY BAFFLES STOCKHOLM SUBURB

FAKE! The real version, believe it or not, is "Tiny pianist wins big competition." Thank you, *Seattle Times*, for that delightful headline.

REAL! Two graduates from the Bellemoor School for Boys are having one heck of a last laugh, according to this 2007 story in the *Metro*. Two years before the article, the guys pulled a bit of a prank with some weed killer, drawing an enormous phallus in a field on school grounds.

The joke was discovered, and the grass was reseeded, but not before Microsoft Virtual Earth took satellite snapshots of the property.

School officials were annoyed that the penis was sullying the online "image" of the institution, but there seemed to be nothing to be done about it.

REAL! The 2011 headline from Sweden's *The Local* went extremely viral, inducing chuckles the world over. It seems that the headline is a bit overstated—it's really not that much of a mystery.

Like our boys from Bellemoor, somebody had fun mowing a giant penis shape into a meadow in a luxurious Stockholm neighborhood. The perpetrators, once again, had perfect timing, and a satellite picture was taken of the penis, which was about the size of a tennis court.

The field phallus has long since grown over, but the Internet image lives on, apparently "baffling" Swedes like crazy.

BREAKING NEWS

Lawsuit: nipple in my spinach dip

RUBBER NIPPLE FOUND IN CODFISH

History is made as nipple is found on foot

FAKE! If you found a nipple in your dip, would you be grossed out, or delighted by the surprise? You know, like the toy in a Cracker Jack box.

In fact, a similar version to this story happened. In 2012, New York's *Daily News* ran the headline: "Lawsuit: animal toe in my spinach dip." Poor Manhattanite Andrew Brodsky was chowing on some spinach dip and felt "something sharp" in his mouth. He spit it out and discovered the toe, nail still attached.

REAL! Not sure why it was big news, but the *Boston Daily Globe* thought so in 1927. A large codfish caught off of Nantucket was discovered to have the tip of a baby's nursing bottle (a.k.a. "nipple") in its belly.

REAL! Supernumerary breast tissue, or "extra nipples," is actually a fairly common condition (just ask Mark Wahlberg and Tilda Swinton). But these bonus nips have never before been known to appear below the waist, as this 2011 article in *The Sun* points out.

Enter a new case and subsequent study in the *Dermatology Journal*, in which a twenty-two-year-old woman was discovered with a fully developed nipple and its accompanying glands on the sole of her foot.

Can't get any further below the waist than that!

Deer vomit is bad for the environment

BURPING COWS ARE KILLING THE PLANET

Kangaroo farts linked to lower emissions

FAKE! You might need to contact an expert to be sure, but as far as I know, deer vomit is not bad for the environment at all.

There are plenty of headlines about surprising things being non-green, however, such as "Illegal immigration is bad for the environment" from ABC News, "Tofu is bad for the environment, finds food study" from Scotland's *Herald*, "Divorce bad for the enivronment: study" from Australia's ABC Online, and this oddly specific one from the *Bangor Daily News*: "Washing off engine with garden hose is bad for the environment."

REAL! The *St. Petersburg Times* might have been a *little* dramatic with the wording of this 2007 lead line, but it is right about the fact that methane produced from the belching of cattle represents a significant percentage of greenhouse gas emissions.

Research teams in England, Japan, and the United States are hard at work trying to find a way to make cows burp less.

REAL! The 2008 story was featured on the news website of Raidió Teilifís Éireann, or RTÉ, a public broadcasting service in Ireland.

The story follows a climate change debate in Australia, in which it is acknowledged that kangaroos produce far less methane from passing gas (out of either end) than do cattle and sheep. Therefore, a group of scientists (in the minority) are waging a campaign to get Australians to farm-raise and eat kangaroo meat as a greener alternative.

'HUMAN BARBIE' BUYS 7-YEAR-OLD DAUGHTER BOOB JOB FOR HER BIRTHDAY

Dad performs boob job on daughter as 18th b'day gift

MAN GIFTS 97-YEAR OLD GREAT-GRANDMOTHER WITH BOOB JOB

REAL! I wish this one were fake.

Britain's Sarah Burge, the self-titled "Human Barbie," shocked plenty of people in 2011 when she gave her seven-year-old daughter Poppy a boob job for her birthday.

It would help to note, as the *Metro* headline didn't, that it was only a "voucher" for the surgery, and that poor little Poppy would have to wait until she's sixteen to redeem it. Burge has spent more than three-quarters of a million dollars on her own cosmetic "enhancements," in a lifelong quest to look like Barbie.

Poppy was quoted in the article to say, "I wanted a new computer, a holiday and a voucher for surgery. When I got it all, it was a dream come true. I can't wait to be like mummy with big boobs."

REAL! The 2012 article in the *Pune Mirror* quotes the dad, California's Dr. Michael Niccole, as saying there's "nothing odd about it."

Apparently, Brittani had been nagging her dad for the operation for over a year. The elder Niccole said, "You can go to war at 18. You can vote at that age, so why not have cosmetic surgery?"

The good doctor also performed cosmetic surgery on his daughter Charm, converting her "outie" belly button into an "innie."

FAKE! Though it would make for a touching story, wouldn't it?

As of presstime, the oldest woman to receive breast augmentation surgery was indeed a great-grandmother, but an immature eighty-four years old at the time. I know we can do better.

SWALLOWS, SURVIVES . . .

An excellent way to recover from all that senseless object-swallowing death (see "Swallows, Dies . . .") is to read up on all of the miraculous object-swallowing survival stories.

WOMAN SWALLOWS 224 ODD BITS OF HARDWARE, LIVES

Warsaw Union, February 16, 1935

In another classic case of what-was-she-thinking, a Nyack, New York, woman swallowed an amazing amount of detritus, including bed springs, a meat skewer, teaspoons, pins, and tire chains. She miraculously survived to tell the tale.

WOMAN SWALLOWS ENTIRE CANTEEN OF CUTLERY

South Africa's _Independent Online_, October 29, 2009

A full seventy-eight forks and spoons were found in a fifty-two-year-old Netherlands woman's stomach when she went to the doctor complaining of stomach pains (go figure). Doctors were able to remove the lot, and she walked away, healthy as ever.

INFANT SWALLOWS SCREWDRIVER, LIVES

Calgary Daily Herald, October 31, 1933

Considering the fact that people routinely die after swallowing something much smaller, it's amazing that fourteen-month-old Donald Cundell was able to run a household tool through his system. As the _Herald_ put it, "nature provided its own cure, and the screwdriver was recovered." Oh, good! The _screwdriver_ was recovered!

BABY SWALLOWS 46 TACKS, LIVES

Chicago Tribune, June 13, 1919

You'd think after the first two or three, he'd be inclined to cut it out. But nope, forty-six tacks, down the hatch. I bet he bragged about it for the rest of his life.

DOG SWALLOWS FLAG POLE!; PUPPY SURVIVES SWALLOWING 113 PENNIES; PUPPY SWALLOWS A FOOT LONG DRUM STICK AND SURVIVES; DOG SWALLOWS LARGE RUBBER DUCKY AND SURVIVES; DOG SWALLOWS BUTCHER KNIFE BUT SURVIVES WITH OPERATION; DOG SWALLOWS METAL WRENCH AND LIVES TO BARK ABOUT IT

Post Chronicle, October 2, 2011; CBS News, September 23, 2010; Gather.com, February 14, 2011; AOL News, December 30, 2010; *Baltimore Afro-American*, March 3, 1973; *Nashua Telegraph*, February 14, 1986

There are many more examples, proving that when it comes to swallowing strange stuff, dogs are hardier than people.

PYTHON SWALLOWS QUEEN-SIZED ELECTRIC BLANKET

ABC News, July 19, 2006

Houdini, a 60-pound, 12-foot Burmese python must have accidentally tangled up his rabbit dinner with his electric blanket. He swallowed the whole thing, including the control box and cord. Surgeons pulled the blanket out, and Houdini went home healthy.

BOY SWALLOWS ROCKET, SURVIVES BLAST IN CHEST

Boston Globe, January 9, 1971

It was in the *Globe*, so it must be true. What Denmark's Vagn Larsen was thinking when he ingested a live firework, I'll never guess.

BOY SWALLOWS BALL-POINT PEN, SUES FOR $25,000

Chicago Tribune, October 24, 1962

Now *that* is the spirit!

Beserk police officer kills four men in bras

TALL TEXAS BLONDE SLUGS JAILER, FLEES IN PANTIES

MAN 'HIGH ON BATH SALTS' ARRESTED IN BRA, PANTIES, ACCUSED OF STABBING GOAT

REAL! The 1963 article from the *Pittsburgh Post-Gazette* reads like a brilliant scene from a classic movie.

Six-foot-tall Millie Jones told her Idaho jailer that she was ready for her shower. When the sixty-two-year-old guard opened her cell, she clobbered him on the head with a shirt sleeve that she'd filled with soap, grabbed his keys, and locked him inside.

Not content to just try and get away, the half-naked blonde found her way to her boyfriend's cell, worked the complicated lock, and freed him. They jumped through a window and shimmied down a fire escape. Jones flagged down a startled driver, and she and her boyfriend took his car and drove off into the sunset.

REAL! It's pretty clear that Mark Thompson of Alum Creek, West Virginia, had a more interesting Saturday night than you did. According to the article in Australia's *Herald Sun*, police found Thompson in women's lingerie, raving and waving a knife over a recently stabbed pygmy goat.

Thompson told officers he was high and wasn't in his "right mind." He was charged with cruelty to animals.

BREAKING NEWS

Florida police searching for heavyset ninja

Stoner ninjas attack pizza deliveryman

Man wrestles crazed ninja kangaroo after it invades family home

REAL! According to the 2009 Fox News article, the criminal should be easy to spot: ninja garb and a "visible potbelly."

Apparently, he tried to steal two ATM machines, both times unsuccessfully. Perhaps it's all just a belated tribute to Chris Farley.

FAKE! It's made-up, but the real version is even better. The 2012 *USA Today* headline reads, "Ninjas attack medical marijuana deliveryman," and an even more descriptive one from CBS News goes a little something like this: "Medical marijuana deliveryman robbed by baton-wielding ninjas in West Covina." The poor guy was making a cannabis delivery when he was ambushed and the pot was taken.

I'm sure they hit the pizza deliveryman next.

REAL! The *Times of London* told this exciting 2009 tale of a "hero in torn underwear."

The awesomely named Beat Ettlin was asleep in his Canberra, Australia, home when a massive kangaroo smashed through his bedroom window and proceeded to jump up and down on the bed, with his wife and nine-year-old daughter still under the covers. The bed collapsed under the animal's weight, which started frantically trying to escape, smashing against the wall and smearing blood everywhere.

Then it bounded down the hall to Ettlin's son's bedroom, and he decided enough was enough. He got the 6-foot-tall beast in a *headlock*, wrestled it to the front of the house, opened the front door, and kicked it outside.

That's what I call taking care of business.

BEIJING OLYMPICS
MENU TO INCLUDE
"DOG'S BRAIN" SOUP

**Prosecutor: Houston
restaurant served eyeball soup**

**Penis stew turns
woman into
vegetarian**

REAL! The 2008 article from Newstrack India helpfully pointed out to tourists that dog brains could, in fact, be served to you in China.

They don't stop there. They also mention that you might find starfish, deep-fried, skinned lizards, rabbit heads, seahorse skewers, donkey penis, dung beetles, silk worms, and horse stew on the menu.

Hungry yet?

FAKE! Never happened, but you can find lots of examples of newspapers and magazines suggesting recipes for "eyeball soup."

Of course, there are no real eyeballs in the soup—only creatively prepared olives, grapes, etc.—and the concoction is suggested for Halloween fun.

REAL! It's impossible to blame the South African woman for going meatless after what happened to her. According to the *Independent Online*, the Pretoria hospital worker went to the cafeteria for lunch and selected the goulash.

When she attempted to bite into the "meat" in the stew, she found it was too tough. She inspected it with a couple of coworkers and determined that it was a penis. She submitted it for analysis, but, as the article claims, "Because it had been cooked, it could not be established whether the penis was from a human or an animal."

Since then, she's just had no taste for meat.

DAD ACCIDENTALLY PLAYS PORN INSTEAD OF "THE SMURFS" AT CHILD'S BIRTHDAY PARTY

Theater shows children adult film "Wet n' Frosty" instead of Megamind cartoon

OOPS: TEACHER ACCIDENTALLY GAVE SELF-MADE SEX TAPE TO 5TH GRADERS

REAL! The *Winnipeg Free Press* ran the article on an apparently slow news day in 2012. A Utah dad suffered embarrassment (and a lot of parents suffered awkward questions from their kids) when he connected his laptop to a projector at his kid's birthday party and treated them to some porn.

The furtive father made things worse for himself by declaring to police that someone must have tampered with the *Smurfs* DVD he'd rented. The DVD was analyzed and found to be in good order, whereas the man's laptop did in fact have plenty of porn on it.

Judging it an accident, police decided he'd been punished enough and leveled no charges at him.

FAKE! Thankfully for little Billy, it never happened. He didn't get away scot-free, though. In 2010 NPR ran this headline: "Theater showed children 'Saw 3D' instead of cartoon."

You can imagine the surprise of kids and parents alike at a Revere, Massachusetts, screening of *Megamind*, when the bloody opening scene of gorefest *Saw 3D* came on the screen. The movie played for several minutes before the error was corrected, exposing the little ones to plenty of carnage.

By the way, *Wet n' Frosty* is the name of an actual snowboarding-themed porn movie.

REAL! A California fifth-grade teacher learned the hard way that she needed to brush up on her editing skills when she accidentally distributed a sex tape of herself to the whole class.

The 2009 CBS News story reported that the DVD was meant to be a compilation of memories from the school year. Instead, she created an indelible new memory for her students.

Twinkie explosion wrecks seals

TWINKIE AIRLIFT HEADED FOR SOLDIERS IN SAUDI DESERT

NO HO-HO: TWINKIE SHORTAGE ON THE WAY

FAKE! It ain't real, but I still suggest you get your seals checked anytime you experience a Twinkie explosion.

The pretend headline is awfully similar to a real one from a 1950 issue of the *Los Angeles Times*: "Twink explosion wrecks Seals, 5–3." In those days, a minor league baseball team called the Hollywood Stars was immensely popular. The Stars were colloquially known as the "Twinks," and on this particular occasion, the team beat the San Francisco Seals in the Pacific Coast League. The league boasted a slew of colorful, now-defunct teams, including the Sacramento Solons, the Portland Beavers, and the Oakland Oaks.

REAL! The *Sacramento Bee* ran this touching story about the flood of letters coming into the Continental Baking Company offices in 1991 from U.S. soldiers fighting abroad in Operation Desert Storm. They decided to send *one million* Twinkies to American forces in the Middle East.

Please tell me the crates were labeled "Operation Dessert Storm."

REAL! This funny-titled article ran in 2000 in the *Cincinnati Enquirer*. It relayed, in a rather alarmist tone, that a trucker strike threatened to deprive "Twinkie lovers from Maine to Washington, D.C." of the spongy, creamy cakes. It also cautioned constituents to stock up on Ding Dongs, Fruit Pies, Ring Dings, and Devil Dogs.

It was a scary time.

NAPLES MAN ARRESTED AT BANK CLAIMS HE'S CIA DIRECTOR, HALF ORANGUTAN

Man accused of having sex with donkey says prostitute transformed herself into a donkey

BELMONT WOMAN ARGUES THAT SHE STABBED HER HUSBAND BECAUSE HE IS A "TOILET DEMON SENT FROM MARS"

REAL! Police in Florida got the tip that a man parked in front of a bank was waving a gun around, reports this 2012 story in the *Naples Daily News*. They went to investigate, found fifty-one-year-old Mark Loescher, and asked him to get out of the car.

That's when things got weird. He refused to get off the phone, he said, because he is half-orangutan and needed to call the "Fusion Center" about his "monkey blood."

When they forced him out of the car, he objected, saying he was the director of the CIA. He went on to claim that he is Elvis Presley's brother and close friends with George W. Bush.

He was arrested.

REAL! The 2011 story in the *Zimbabwe Mail* represents the greatest excuse for committing a crime that I've ever heard.

When Zvishavane, Zimbabwe, police found Sunday Moyo having sex with a tied-up donkey in his front yard, he acted as shocked as they were. In court, he was recorded as saying, "Your worship, I only came to know that I was being intimate with a donkey when I got arrested." He explained that he had hired a prostitute in the city and brought her home, and that she had used magic to transform herself into a donkey when police arrived.

Moyo went on to announce that he was in love with the donkey. The judge ordered that he undergo a psychiatric evaluation.

FAKE! I had fun coming up with that one. I've been threatened with a stabbing numerous times because of my "toilet habits." Sometimes I think men *are* from Mars, and women are from Bed Bath & Beyond.

Man tried to use $1,000,000 bill at Walmart

MAN TRIES TO USE GLITTERY PINK DILDO TO ROB SEATTLE CONVENIENCE STORE

Man in Brazil tries to use Jack Nicholson's face to open bank account

REAL! In a serious case of wishful thinking, a Lexington, North Carolina, man tried to buy a vacuum cleaner and a microwave with a forged million-dollar bill at the local Walmart in 2011, says Winston-Salem's WXII-TV.

I can see the look on the cashier's face now. The man insisted that the bill was real, even after police arrived. (The largest bill in circulation is $100.)

And, if you had a *real* million-dollar bill, would your first purchase be a vacuum cleaner?

FAKE! There have been reports of dildo-wielding criminals, but most of these are cases of bizarre assaults.

There have been plenty of strange convenience-store-robbery weapon choices as well, such as the Florida man who tried (and failed) to rob a corner store with a PlayStation controller, and my favorite: the Arizona woman who tried to rob a Chevron with a toy penguin.

REAL! Ricardo Sergio Freire de Barros does not look a thing like Jack Nicholson, reports the 2012 story in the *Dallas Morning News*. And yet, he tried to pass off a fake ID bearing the iconic Oscar-winner's mug as he opened a bank account in Boa Viagem, Brazil.

The impostor was already under investigation for opening bogus accounts and maxing their credit limits when he pulled the stunt. I wonder whose picture he used for those. Tom Cruise? Lady Gaga?

Man wanted yin-yang tattoo, got penis

NEW HAMPSHIRE BULLIES TATTOO PENIS ON CLASSMATE'S FACE

Penis tattoo leads to permanent erection

REAL! An Ipswich, Australia, man asked a friend to give him a tattoo on his back of a yin-yang symbol and a dragon. The friend, inexplicably, decided to give him a tattoo of a 15-inch penis instead, says the 2010 Special Broadcasting Service story.

The "artist" was charged with assault.

FAKE! The Concord, New Hampshire, bullies *did* force a fourteen-year-old kid to get a tattoo of a penis, but thankfully it was not on his face.

They told the kid that they would stop picking on him forever if he would consent to the tattoo, and when he still resisted, they threatened him with bodily harm. For his trouble, the boy with self-esteem issues and learning disabilities wound up with a cartoon penis tattooed *on his butt*, along with the words "POOP DICK."

Keep it classy, New Hampshire.

REAL! A twenty-one-year-old Iranian man decided to tattoo a Persian slogan meaning "good luck" on his penis, and wound up with more luck than he bargained for, according to this 2012 ABC News article.

A strange, internal bleeding reaction to the inking caused the man's penis to enter a permanent state of semi-erection.

Reportedly, the man canceled plans to surgically correct the reaction when he realized that he was still able to achieve a full erection and lead a normal sex life, and subsequently enjoyed the newfound bulk in his boxers.

Man takes woman out on date while friend robs her house

MAN LEAVES MOVIE, STEALS DATE'S CAR

Man goes on blind date, has kidney stolen

REAL! A gullible Miami woman was excited when she met a hot Italian guy at a party, and thrilled when he asked her out on a lunch date to Applebee's, according to this 2012 story from Alabama's *Corner News.*

The date, however, was horrible. It was awkward, and at the end of it, he swiped her cell phone and left her with the bill. Imagine the way she fumed as she drove home, only to discover that her house had been broken into and nearly $5,000 worth of her property had been stolen.

The larcenous lothario was eventually caught.

REAL! What's up with all these philandering Florida felons?

Michael Pratt went to the movies with his date in Tampa, the 2011 NBC News story explains, then stood up in the middle and told her he needed to grab something from the car. She handed him the keys. When Pratt didn't return, she went outside to find her 2012 Ford Focus missing. She called him, and he just laughed at her.

Four days later, he ditched the car, which was a rental, in a Wal-mart parking lot. He was found and arrested.

FAKE! Totally not true. But remember all those urban legends? Someone accepts a drink in a bar from a stranger and wakes up the next day in a bathtub packed with ice and one less kidney?

None of it ever happened. But I remember spreading the rumor myself in high school.

Welcome freshman: 29-year old porn star allowed to go back to high school

HIGH SCHOOL BANS STUDENT'S PORN STAR PROM DATE

IT'S OFFICIAL: YOU CAN BE A PORN STAR AND TEACH HIGH SCHOOL STUDENTS

FAKE! But if you want to write a romantic comedy screenplay with me based on this premise, call my agent.

REAL! Eighteen-year-old Minnesota high school student Mike Stone hatched a plan in 2012 to snag a prom date that would turn heads: ask porn stars via Twitter. He scored when adult film actress Megan Piper agreed to be his date.

If you ask me, Stone's gambit showed that he has a lot of positive qualities: creativity, determination, original thinking, and a fantastic sense of humor. However, representatives of his school district didn't agree, reprimanding him and putting the kibosh on the scheme.

Perhaps the biggest loser in the whole buzzkill is porn actress Piper, who missed her own prom and looked forward to making it up. She was quoted to say, "I don't plan to show up butt naked or anything. I'm going to wear a pretty prom dress."

REAL! Australia's *Courier-Mail* issued this sweeping decree in 2011, referring to high school teacher Benedict Garrett, who, when it was revealed that he moonlights as Johnny Anglais, a stripper and porn star, was allowed to keep his job by his East London employer. The best part: the muscle-bound Brit, who appeared in movies such as *European Honeyz 4*, was head of sex education at the school.

I guess he's qualified!

IT'S UP TO MAN WHETHER TO WEAR PANTIES OR NOT

Straight men don't wear panties

Men in Detroit wear panties

FAKE! The real headline from a 1950 *Spokane Daily Chronicle* is "It's up to man whether to wear mustache or not." It's an illuminating article that says if a husband grows a 'stache and his wife doesn't like it, she should just sit and spin.

REAL! The voice behind this silly 1982 article from North Carolina's *Times-News* is not some big, masculine lout, but celebrity columnist Ann Landers.

A concerned guy had written in to complain that she called every guy who wears panties, garters, girdles, and/or pantyhose a transvestite. He remarked that he had chronic back problems and that wearing a girdle and women's pantyhose under his slacks eases his discomfort considerably.

In her reply, Miss Landers took the rather crude position that *any* man that dons women's underthings for *any* reason is, by definition, a transvestite.

REAL! I love how this 1945 headline from the *St. Petersburg Times* sounds like the opening salvo in an insult war. I wonder if the next day the *Michigan Chronicle* ran something like: "Men in St. Petersburg wet their beds."

In truth, the story was a rather interesting piece of investigative reporting that uncovered the fact that a textile shortage was leading Detroit men to start wearing women's underwear, for lack of cheap alternatives.

My favorite line from the article: "While city officials vehemently denied yesterday that Detroit men were turning sissies, local store clerks assert they are."

FORMER REDHEAD STARTS SYNAGOGUE FOR NYU STUDENTS

Cane toad found in Redhead

SPERM BANK TURNS DOWN REDHEADS

FAKE! That doesn't make any sense. How could you think it was real? Replace the word "redhead" with the word "deadhead" (as in, devotee of the rock band The Grateful Dead) and you have a real headline from the *Albany Times Union*.

REAL! The *Newcastle Herald* featured the story about a man who discovered a cane toad in his garden at his home in the suburb of Redhead, in New South Wales, Australia. The man did just what the newspaper suggested one should do if one finds a cane toad in the garden. Pop it in the freezer.

REAL! The United Kingdom's *Daily Telegraph* reported this story of incorrigible hair-pigment racism by the world's largest sperm bank, Cryos, in Denmark.

The director of the bank, Ole Schou, claimed, "There are too many redheads in relation to demand." However, he did report that redhead-generated sperm are popular in Ireland, where they sell "like hot cakes." That's a nice image. Maple syrup is optional.

BIG BALLS ARE IN FASHION THIS WINTER

Diners with balls head to Serbia's testicle-eating festival

BREAKING NEWS

I KICKED A BURNING TERRORIST SO HARD IN THE BALLS THAT I TORE A TENDON IN MY FOOT

FAKE! That's silly. Big balls are *always* in fashion.

You may have seen this 2011 headline, however, in the *Manila Bulletin*: "The Big Balls are back, and they're dressed up for winter." You've got to give it to them for the attention-grabber of a title, but the article itself is just a reminder that the obstacle course TV series *Wipeout* was coming back for another season, this one snow-themed. Contestants on the show traverse all kinds of challenges, including making it across a row of huge, slippery balls.

REAL! Once a year, in the small village of Ozrem, Serbia, you can take part in the grand tradition of eating testicles, according to this 2010 AOL News story.

The World Testicle Cooking Championship, as it is known, draws a diverse crowd from all over the world, all gathered to compete with their favorite testes-based dish. From donkey balls to shark balls (yes, they have them), the festival seems to know no bounds.

Contact your travel agent today!

REAL! Scotland's *Daily Record* gets the award for craziest headline of all time with this 2007 gem.

Two would-be terrorists enacted a brilliant plan of setting their own car on fire and attempting to drive it into Glasgow Airport. A cab driver witnessed the ensuing fracas and decided to take justice into his own hands. His account of the situation was directly quoted in this headline, which has since achieved legendary status.

SUMO WRESTLER STEALS 200-POUND CASH MACHINE IN MOSCOW

Sumo composer-trombonist plays delightful recital

WOMAN IN SUMO WRESTLER SUIT ASSAULTED HER EX-GIRLFRIEND IN GAY PUB AFTER SHE WAVED AT A MAN DRESSED AS SNICKERS BAR

REAL! It plays out like a scene from a wacky '80s crime movie. Guy walks into a shopping mall in broad daylight with his huge goon trailing behind him. He gestures to a nearby ATM machine; the enormous bruiser rips it out of the ground with his bare hands; and the duo proceed back out of the mall to the getaway car.

The movie scene, however, might not have ended in such ignominy. According to the 2010 Fox News story, by the time they had the machine loaded up and got into the car, police were knocking on the window. The big beefcake turned out to be an amateur sumo wrestler.

The cash machine had about $800 in it.

FAKE! I want there to be a sumo-wrestling trombone-composer. I really do. We'll just have to settle for actual composer-slash-trombonist (tromposer-combonist?) Peter Zummo. See what I did there?

REAL! It's so very weird, and so deliciously real. The headline of the 2010 story from Ireland's *Evening Herald* pretty much says it all.

Things were already on the rocks for two ladies on the evening of a costume party at the George Pub, a popular gay nightspot in Dublin. All it took to set the sumo-dressed woman off was one wave by her ex-lover at a man who was dressed as a giant candy bar. The sumo freaked out, pulled a bottle from inside her costume, and thwonked her ex on the head with it.

Boom. Front-page news.

KILLS WITH . . .

It wasn't Professor Plum in the library with the candlestick. It was something far stranger. Searching newspaper archives, you'll read about a man who killed his rapist with a pickle jar. You'll discover *two* cases of murder by toilet tank lid, and three of murder-by-microwave. People seem to be endlessly creative when it comes to weaponry. Here are some of my favorites:

CALIFORNIA MAN KILLS GIRLFRIEND WITH CANNON

FOX News, March 7, 2012

Protrero, California's Richard Dale Fox was a bit of a history enthusiast, and he was crafting an old-style cannon in his trailer home just north of the Mexico border. The cannon fired in the mobile home, injuring Fox and killing his girlfriend in the next room. A court will decide whether it was murder or an accident.

KILLS WIFE WITH TEACUP

New York Times, December 21, 1937

It seems that William Egan, an apartment super at 102 West 99th Street in Manhattan, was not pleased with the way his wife Bridget cooked a rack of lamb. He grabbed a teacup from the table and flung it at her. It struck her on the forehead, lacerating major blood vessels, and she died.

MAN FALLS, KILLS WIFE WITH CHAINSAW

Sydney Morning Herald, August 5, 2004

A fifty-six-year-old London man was on a ladder, pruning a tree in his yard with a chainsaw. He slipped from the ladder and fell onto his wife, accidentally plunging the chainsaw into her body. Talk about standing in the wrong spot.

WOMAN KILLS HUSBAND WITH A GRENADE

New Straits Times, May 31, 1974

A Bangkok, Thailand, woman, angry that her husband was flirting with other women, decided to do something about it. As he danced with another woman at a party, she took out a grenade, pulled the pin, and *held it against his head*. It exploded, killing him instantly and destroying her hand.

WOMAN KILLS HUSBAND WITH FOLDING COUCH

Reuters, July 9, 2008

A Russian woman, angry with her drunk, layabout husband, kicked the lever of the foldout couch that he was sprawled upon during an argument and walked out of the room. The couch was designed to fold automatically and enveloped the man in its mechanisms, killing him instantly.

ROOSTER KILLS MAN WITH SINGLE KICK

Milwaukee Sentinel, May 19, 1925

You could say that Filipino cockfighting matchmaker Andres Mercado had it coming to him. Immediately after a particularly vicious rooster won a fighting match, it turned on Mercado and struck him in the abdomen. The problem? The cock had a razor-sharp blade attached to each leg. Mercado died within an hour.

ROOKIE COP KILLS MAN WITH TOY GUN

Connecticut's *Record-Journal*, June 17, 1998

My imagination went into overdrive when I spied this headline, trying to conceive of a way to kill somebody with a toy gun. It turns out the editor was guilty of vague wording here—he should have said, "Man pulls toy gun on cop, gets shot with real gun for his trouble."

ABOUT THE AUTHOR

NEIL PATRICK STEWART

Neil Patrick Stewart is a writer, teacher, director, and actor. This is his second book with Adams Media; the first, *Fact. Fact. Bullsh*t!: Learn the Truth and Spot the Lie on Everything from Tequila-Made Diamonds to Tetris's Soviet Roots—Plus Tons of Other Totally Random Facts from Science, History, and Beyond!* hit bookstores in 2011. He has written more than 100 magazine articles for such titles as *Gotham* magazine, *Los Angeles Confidential* magazine, *Vegas* magazine, *USA Today*, and *Delta Sky* magazine. Neil holds an MFA in acting from Harvard/A.R.T. and a BA in theatre from Wesleyan University. He is a founder and faculty member of the groundbreaking nonprofit Performing Arts Project, and a teacher at the internationally acclaimed Heifetz International Music Institute. Neil directed Ovation-recommended *The Elephant Man* for the Mechanicals Theatre Group in Los Angeles, and is the director of the brand-new musical *Volleygirls*. Neil is a former founder and creative director of Back House Productions, which was the birthplace of the smash-hit musical *In the Heights*. As an actor, he was seen in the American Repertory Theatre's *The Onion Cellar* and *Julius Caesar*, and has performed *Caesar* internationally in three tours of France, along with a stint in Bogotá, Colombia. Neil grew up in Fort Worth, Texas, and currently lives in Chicago, New York, and Los Angeles with his wife Monica Raymund. Visit neilpatrickstewart.com and follow him on Twitter @bald.